STRIPPER SHOES

By

Cheryl S. Bartlett, Ph.D.

This book is a work of non-fiction. Names and places have been changed to protect the privacy of all individuals. The events and situations are true.

ISBN: 1-4140-4507-7 (e-book)
ISBN: 1-4140-4505-0 (Paperback)
ISBN: 1-4140-4506-9 (Dust Jacket)

Library of Congress Control Number: 2003098999

This book is printed on acid free paper.

Printed in the United States of America
Bloomington, IN

1stBooks - rev. 01/21/04

Dedicated to Ruth Winsten

ACKNOWLEDGEMENTS

As always, for Maria, Dmitri & Allan

For Howard Stern, stripper aficionado, lesbian enthusiast,
and sentinel of the first amendment

Thank you to

Teresita Flores
John & Susan Fulginiti
Sue Hoffman
Mary Lynn McGee
Mighty Joe Boatman
PHMF
Emily Ratley
Greg R.
Sandi Rosenbloom
Ivan Segal
Aurelie Sheehan
Ron T.
Sabrina Woods

To caring, funny, wise, bitchy women who dance for a living

To my fabulous editor and publicist,
Carol Givner

With much love to my parents, for forgiving me in advance,
My brother, Mike, who prefers to believe this book is fiction,
My sister, Joanna, who is always on my side, no matter what, and
Pompa, and Nani, who said a blessing over all of my query letters

It's the good girls who keep the diaries;
the bad girls never have the time.

— Tallulah Bankhead (1903-1968)

TABLE OF CONTENTS

Stripper Shoes

Beware of all enterprises that require new clothes
— Henry David Thoreau

It's amazing how quickly fear and adrenaline can kill a buzz.

The first time, the trick is to be just drunk enough to take your clothes off in public, but not quite so drunk as to fall off the stage, a complicated balance of blood volume to alcohol that is no simple task for the uninitiated.

My first time, dancing and crawling around half-naked for the amusement of lonely software engineers, programmers and salesmen, I came away with eight bucks, all ones. Still dazed and undecided about whether I should be humiliated or proud, I stepped off the stage to congratulating pats and smiles from other dancers and the DJ.

I suppose that since I can't take it back, I may as well be proud.

Without my glasses, faces around the stage look blurry. From my perspective, it is just as well. I've become completely paranoid about being caught topless on stage by someone from my office. My fears are not entirely unwarranted, with only one strip club in town, it is only a matter of time before some clandestine bachelor party comes up, and there I'll be in all my glory. I can just imagine my boss dragged in by some client or company man to schmooze, looking completely bored and embarrassed until he sees me here.

"Excuse me, Dr. Bartlett, don't I pay you enough?"

Trichotillomania

Until you've lost your reputation, you never realize what a burden it was.

— Margaret Mitchell

None of my fears materialized.

I didn't trip and fall. The clothes came off, though none too gracefully, and, thankfully, no one began a chant of "Put it back on! Put it back on!" Now all I feel is strangely clammy, but clear as a bell and glad to have the audition behind me instead of ahead.

I keep expecting to feel dirty and embarrassed, but so far I don't.

I guess I might feel that way if I had to dance because I had no other choice, if I had to strip to pay the bills. If you ask me, dancing seems a lot less degrading and obnoxious than waiting tables, telephone sales, or cleaning houses turned out to be. Young, poor women, single mothers in particular, are vulnerable and easily targeted by all sorts of distasteful, demeaning jobs.

But they earn a lot more being demeaned as a stripper.

So much has changed, all at once it seemed. I finally wrapped up my degree to start my first real job in a new city. I moved into an apartment temporarily while my family stayed behind to finish out the school year and sell our home of fifteen years.

In hindsight, I recognize the obvious symptoms of a mid-life crisis. I hated my new life. I was miserable, lonely and severely depressed. Out of stress, I had begun to pick compulsively at my left eyebrow until it was almost bald. Every morning, I cried in the shower before leaving for work. It wasn't long before I was crying during work. I couldn't concentrate and couldn't get anything done. As is the popular response to deep, consistent feelings of hopelessness these days, I headed to my neighborhood pharmacy for anti-depressants.

I started with 10 milligrams a day, then 20, and then 40. I stopped picking my eyebrow and cut way down on the obsessing, but I still cried an awful lot. I couldn't seem to help it, though I did try. The pills didn't alleviate my depression, but they did cause dry mouth, excessive sleepiness, and made me physically incapable of achieving an orgasm.

When even masturbation had nothing to offer me, I found myself with too much time to think. What is it that I am looking for? I have my health. I have a husband and kids that I love. I put myself through school from junior college to a Ph.D., and landed an incredible job. While my friends struggled with marriage, divorce, money, illness, fertility, I seemed to have it all covered, and yet there wasn't a dosage high enough to get me through the day.

By the time my family joined me up north, I thought I'd feel better, but instead, I got so much worse. Soon enough, we had moved our whole lives. The kids were in school and we put a down payment on a new house. I was committing myself to something that felt wrong from the beginning, but I know me. Once I had completely committed, I never would have backed off. I'd have to see it through, whatever it took.

At every stage in my life I would think, *once I get to the next stage, then I can finally be myself.* Once I finish my dissertation, once I have Dr. in front of my name, once I get a good job…then I can stop having to prove myself and focus on today.

But that is not what happened. With my new life, came greater responsibilities and bigger bills and more stress and politics simply to maintain them. Whenever I arrived at what I thought was a destination, there were intense personalities and stumbling blocks to negotiate, and so much more pressure to ensure that I did. Stripping would be a potentially irrecoverable deviation from the plan.

I'd always watch when strippers came on TV and think I could do that, but why would I want to? I can't ask any of my friends for advice; I already know what they will say. Stripping is degrading. My parents will be mortified. People will find out, and it will ruin my career. My friends will not understand and I'll have to find a way to hide it from my kids. Among other considerations, my husband will worry about my personal safety.

The thoughts trickled into what had become my lonely, listless, subconscious mind: the dancing, the costumes, the glamour, the excited fear of going through with it — the fear of *not* going through with it. Whatever the reason, I felt inspired and energized for the first time in a very long while. Tired and bored with the obsessively repetitive, sullen, self-deprecating thoughts in my mind, I had a new plan.

I'd revisit my body.

Stripping for Dummies

If I can't dance, I don't want to be part of your revolution
— Emma Goldman (paraphrased)

Strippers always make me think of Starsky and Hutch.

When I conjure up the inner workings of strip clubs, I imagine the seedy nightspot where the hunky pair extracted critical details from their comic relief, street-wise informant, Huggy Bear. In the background, sexy, but dirty-looking, bikini-clad women danced on platforms surrounded by sprinklings of similarly unwashed male extras. Although TV strippers have changed little since the seventies, I've never actually been in a strip club before now, so Starsky and Hutch are all I have to go on.

I scan the local weekly newspaper, the kind with concert information, explicit personals, and gratuitous ads for topless clubs. I find a few contenders, Blinky's, Zoot Allures, and Tinseltown. Blinky's and Tinseltown are farther from my office, which means there is less chance of being recognized, but also a much longer commute after a full day's work. I settle on the Zoot Allures, the solitary strip club nearby that has been in business for over twenty years. Something of a landmark, it was the subject of local debate and allowed to remain, but tightly regulated. I call the number listed in the ad with a coupon for two dollars off admission. The man on the phone says to come in and apply anytime during business hours, 2:00 PM to 2:00 AM.

Following my downloaded map directions carefully, I arrive Sunday night about half past nine. I forgot my coupon, but deflect the six-dollar cover charge by asking the doorman whether the club is currently hiring dancers. Although I know that strip clubs offset the notoriously high turnover of dancers by constantly hiring new ones, I make a point of asking because it seems like the least awkward way of communicating my extremely awkward intentions.

The doorman, Jim, is a big guy about twenty-two years old. Although friendly enough, he ignores my feeble attempts to make conversation as he rounds up the people and documents necessary to begin the application process. He seems overly cautious toward me, but it could just be my imagination. Maybe it's because of my clothes. I'm not dressed the way I imagine stripper job applicants on television might dress. Maybe it's my age; he might think I look too old to be a stripper. I refuse to entertain this idea for long because if I start thinking that way, I'll lose my nerve altogether.

Before I have much time to imagine all the club employees snickering in the back at the prospect of me as a stripper, Jim asks for some identification. Sadly, this request is unrelated to any possibility, however remote, that I might be underage. Photocopying identification is strictly formal procedure. I could look sixty and they would still insist.

The club is dimly lit, but not too dark. The bar, with an adjacent pool table and scattered tables nearby, looms immediately beyond where the doorman takes the entrance fee. To the right is a large room with three stages, each surrounded by seating. There is no seating at the bar itself, presumably to keep customers from stationing themselves there instead of near the dancers.

The atmosphere is upscale. The furniture does not strike me as new, but not worn either. The tables are clean and free of obvious scratches or gouges. The seating consists of neatly upholstered chairs in an easy to clean, heavy-duty vinyl, and high-backed fabric chairs, both in the ladies restroom area and in the smoking lounge. I see no clearly identifiable place where Starsky and Hutch might situate themselves to advance an investigation, yet the interiors do seem vaguely familiar.

On the side nearest to the door is a raised platform that runs along the length of a mirrored wall where small tables are set up with chairs facing the mirror. Table dances are performed here, and cameras, presumably for security, are strategically placed around the club. On the opposite wall, behind one of the stages, is a short set of stairs with a guardrail in front of it, leading to the curtained entrance of the dressing room. To the left of the bar is a separate smoking lounge with one stage and two pool tables.

I'm sent over to the bartender, who hands me a long set of paperwork. I'm stunned at how detailed it is. Even as I feel guilty for thinking it, I wonder if these strippers are capable of completing such complicated forms. I'm pretty sure that I'm not.

I do the best I can in a hurry, and when I'm done I deliver them to Kurt, the club manager. Kurt gives me some rules to look over so that I can finish completing the paperwork. Page after page describe in detail the rules for dancers, mostly based on state law. Foremost, no drugs or prostitution are allowed. Despite the very creative spelling and grammar, the remainder of the rules is fairly specific, and occasionally graphically descriptive.

I may not touch my genitals or breasts. A caveat to this rule - apparently I *am* allowed to use my upper arms for the purpose of squeezing my breasts together. I may not touch the customer when I have my top off. I must remain at arm's length from the customers when on stage. I may not simulate masturbation, oral sex, or any other sex acts that might occur to me given enough time. I may not pick up a tip with my "rear," not that I could, even if I wanted to.

Rule number 21 is my favorite, *Please dress in an appealing and sexy manor (sic). Our customers would stay at home if they wanted to see a girl dressed like an old housewife.* There are a variety of regulations about drinking, smoking, disputes with other employees, and punctuality. No one can leave for the night until the dressing room is clean.

There are some disturbing rules, too. For instance, *You cannot use your mouth to take a tip if the customer is touching it.* Which part of this rule is critical? Can I take a tip with my mouth if a customer is *not* touching it? *Do not insert your finger or any part of your body in a customer's drink.* I could have gone my whole life happily ignorant of the need to post either of these two regulations.

Despite a few odd rules that I can only suspect must have stemmed from some prior bizarre and hopefully isolated incident, when I consider the vulnerability of the situation, and the true need for people (particularly the dancers) to respect each other's space, the rules are straightforward, make sense, and do not seem especially oppressive.

I'm surprised to read that dancers of age are allowed to buy and accept drinks. Later, when I pay $6.50 for a small glass of white zinfandel, it becomes clear why management does not require total abstinence. According to my list, which I was required to sign, date, and return, we are allowed to accept a customer's offer to buy a drink, but it is strictly forbidden to solicit one. I have my doubts about enforcement on this one.

Kurt has someone call a dancer to the bar so she might show me around and explain the job further. "Delilah" is bubbly and greets me with warmth. Cynic that I am, I assume Kurt must have called over the very nicest dancer to show me the ropes. She is slender, athletic, not too tall, and is wearing a silver halter-top and matching low-rise stretchy bell-bottom pants. On her feet are enormous platform, glittery, high-heeled shoes.

I admire the piercings in her bottom lip and belly button and she begins to show me around.

"The dressing room is where we change costumes and freshen up between sets." Right away it's *we,* and I like it. Delilah shows me the contents of her locker as she goes over the basic guidelines, some that are on the list, and some that are not.

"I'm nineteen; I started dancing the day after my eighteenth birthday. This is my favorite place so far. I'm from Michigan, and you would not believe the crazy shit that goes on there!"

I listen, nodding and smiling.

"Guys would get drunk and rowdy and whip their dicks out, and fuck no, if you think anybody ever does anything about it! And it's no big surprise because the girls do *everything*, which means if you want to make money then you have to do everything, too. Everywhere you turn, someone is trying to fuck you or fuck you over. You can work twice as hard and they'll pay you less than minimum wage, then have the balls to cheat you out of it, make up reasons to dock your pay or short your check, thinking you are too stupid to count! It's not like that here, but it is pretty strict. You can't get too crazy, or the club could get fined and you'll get fired. So you don't make as much money as you would somewhere else. Here, if a guy looks at you funny, and you want him gone, you tell a bouncer and he's out of here. That hardly ever happens; they behave themselves for the most part. Mostly salesmen and techies."

She talks a mile a minute, and I begin to wonder if she is on speed or cocaine. Given my preconceived notions, I jump to that conclusion until she picks up a little jar of tiny, fruit-shaped candy, and dips her hand into it every three or four minutes. Her eyes are perfectly clear, and she has the bounce-off-the-walls exuberance of a little girl who has had too much sugar.

Delilah shows me some basic moves and reminds me twice not to slam down on my knees or they will fill with a fluid that will eventually require surgical drainage. She knows this, because she has just recovered from having that particular procedure done. Delilah goes through her locker and shows off some of her costumes. "You want your T-bar to be skimpy, but it needs to have a little triangle or something at the top to cover your butt crack." Evidently, a T-bar is the same thing as a G-string, but, as she explained, with some additional detail or fabric to cover the cleft of the buttocks, which by club rule, city ordinance, or state law, must not be visible. Typical thong underwear looks like grandma's underpants next to these babies.

She turns away and bends over — all the way over — looking intently at me from between her long legs, "Oh, and you want to shave everything even back here too, or the customers will talk about your hairy ass behind your back and who needs that, right?" Her voice is a little scratchy. She has a prominent mid-western accent, but with a deep, sexy quality to it. While I stand there trying to be only an observer, an objective bystander chronicling this decorum-free zone, I find myself so taken by her self-assurance and character that I have to stop, make a quick mental note about her presence, and refocus on what she is telling me.

"This really is a great place to work. Most of the dancers here are super nice. There are some bitches, like anywhere, but for the most part the girls are great. See that purse? It's been sitting there all day. You have to be careful because some girls will come through just to steal and then move on. Lock everything up. You'll have to wait until a lot of other dancers quit before you can get your own locker. Find someone who will share with you or lock up your bag and try to keep it out of the way. Are you going to audition tonight?"

She's talking so fast that I can barely keep up with all the information. What happened to *we*? I have to audition? I say no, I want my first impression to be a good one. Since I didn't shave my legs this morning, much less any other private parts soon to be public, I'll have to come back. For some reason, I hadn't even considered having to audition. I guess I assumed that if you wanted to strip, you just signed on and showed up. I get a little panicky at the thought that I might not get hired. I imagine falling down at my audition in those enormous shoes.

"Have you ever fallen down in those shoes?" I ask.

"Oh no, Honey," she giggles at me, "Don't worry, you won't fall down, you get used to them."

She begins to tell me how *we* make money.

"First of all, you need a name. And don't tell anyone your real name. I mean, you can tell the dancers your real name, but then they'll end up using it sometimes, and you don't want that, so it's just best to stick with your stage name." I realize that I hadn't given this much thought either. Maybe I've been overly focused on my one big concern up to this point.

I am going to be naked in front of a room full of strangers.

Clearly this is far more complicated than I would have expected based on my extensive viewing of seventies television. I don't care much for the very stage-y names like Emotion or Vanity (besides, these were already taken), but because Delilah is steadily introducing me around, I feel under the gun to come up with something.

"What about Diva?" I interject, which, by the way, is the name of my Great Dane who is currently boarded with my other two dogs, a boxer and a lab-chow mix, until we get settled in and find a more permanent place to live. I dismiss my own suggestion before they could even respond. Roxy chimes in, "If I were a blonde like you, I'd call myself 'Champagne'." This doesn't sound like me at all. The thought that keeps coming back to me during this stripper name brainstorming session is that my mother would consider all of these names to be very affected. Like Lauren Bacall's voiceover on commercials for cat food, stripper names are affected. As if, when my mother finds out about this, her big issue will be with the name I choose. Finally, I settle on "Trinity" after the heroine in the high-grossing nerd favorite, The Matrix.

"Are you married? Do you have kids?" I would be asked these two questions hundreds of times during my brief tenure. I answer affirmatively, "Yes, I have a boy, Dmitri, he's sixteen, and a girl, Maria, she's almost twelve."

"Don't tell them you're married or have kids. They want the fantasy. They want to believe that you might go home with them. If they want your phone number ask for theirs instead or give them a fake one. When they find out it's fake, they'll just pretend they didn't try to call. And don't ever go out with customers. Some girls here do, but I think they are out of their freaking minds. But it doesn't matter what you tell them, just tell them what they want to hear. And look into their eyes. Don't forget to stare into their eyes."

Delilah's turn comes up, so I sit at the stage and watch her dance. She is very flexible and does the splits on stage. I figure I will be just fine if I don't try that myself, but when I see her hop up and spin her body around on the poles with a sexy confidence and flair, I'm more than a little envious. Also, she bangs her boots very loudly on the stage floor as she flips herself around several times during her performance. It looks - and sounds - to me that she is slamming her knees down on the stage just the way she told me not to.

There are too few customers, and Delilah looks bored. I can see that she is phoning in her usual routine and could be saving her energy for later if things get busier, or for her own evening out after the shift. I get up to ask Kurt about auditioning. We arrange my audition for the following Wednesday night at eight-thirty.

The Stripper Diet

An ecdysiast is one who - or that which - sheds its skin.
In vulgar parlance, a stripper. But I'm not a stripper.
At these prices, I'm an ecdysiast!"

— *Gypsy Rose Lee*

Other than the secretary, I am usually the first one in the office in the morning. I like the quiet and the stillness of the building as I make a pot of coffee. I can take my time getting ready for the hours that follow. It's my favorite part of the work day, the only time I don't feel completely miserable and out of place. My problem lately is that I have so little to get ready for. I find myself sitting around waiting for work to do. There isn't enough to keep me busy all week, except on Friday afternoon, when I get loaded down to keep me working all weekend. Until then, I have plenty of time to daydream and worry about my audition.

It's not as if I've spent my life dreaming of becoming a stripper. Exotic dancing is a fairly new obsession. Sixteen years ago as a single, teenage mother broke and struggling to get through school, stripping would have made sense. Despite the genuine financial need, not to mention a much younger and more flexible body, I never would have dared. I know what people would have said about me if I had.

Years later, married with two kids of my own, a good job in a new city no less than a thousand miles away from anyone who knows me, I go and pull a stunt like this. Whatever it is that is nagging at me isn't one thing in particular, or an impulse, but more like a collection of circumstances.

Having always been a person more cerebral than physical, I tend to live a pleasant, if sedentary life firmly stationed in my mind. In spite of my recent stress-induced weight gain, for the first time in my life, I appreciate my body. I want to get to know it better. To shed the extra pounds and become more in touch with my body, I suppose I could start jogging or take up yoga. Like most people, I've begun

15

many different exercise programs, each regimen less satisfying than the one before. I dread the thought of another expensive membership or stupid exercise videotape, and, of course, the guilt that comes with not using either of them.

When I turned thirty, along with the extra weight, my hormones went crazy. I began to feel not just more sexual, but sensual. I have a new confidence in my body that I couldn't have even imagined before, and now I revel in. I would hate to waste this feeling.

I'm not yet exactly sure what it is that I am trying to shed, or more accurately, to be stripped of. My diplomas, my sensible family car, and my middle class home on a quiet cul de sac - all the evidence I've collected over the years to appear worthy and respectable. I have managed to convince myself that these symbols of stability somehow buy me enough credibility to get away with this.

I completed my degree, landed my dream job, put my house on the market, pulled my children out of school, and moved my family to a new city. I couldn't understand why I didn't feel energized and relieved by these changes and milestones. I dismissed every opportunity to listen to my intuition, and ignored every red flag, chalking them up to my inexperience and insecurity.

Everything felt wrong from the start, but after all that, I couldn't just up and change my mind. Despite my steadfast dedication to stay the course and give my new career a chance, my subconscious would find a way to intercede on my behalf. I didn't have the guts to take control of my own life, so I let the ecdysiast in me sabotage it.

Re-thinking My Jewelry

It is never too late — in fiction or in life — to revise
— Nancy Thayer

I need a new image.

Until Delilah showed me her wardrobe, I thought I could rummage through my underwear drawer for some sexy bras and panties. I had hoped that my collection of purchased, but rarely worn lingerie would be sufficient to get me through, at the very least, an audition, maybe even a shift or two. No dice. They were either too complicated, too frumpy by comparison, or see-through, which is against the rules. I want to look sexy and professional - professional stripper, that is - and of course, conform to the posted guidelines.

My first priority is to simplify my debut by wearing something that can be easily removed, as gracefully as possible under the circumstances. I need to go shopping.

After leaving my office for the day, I check out "Fascinations", a fairly soft-core adult store that carries novelties, lubricants, some porno stuff in the back, and a few sexy dancer outfits. I don't want to spend a lot of money, so I grab a stretchy, black and white checkered sheath-type dress that was packaged in plastic and hung on the wall along with fancy stockings and accessories. It's a bargain at $14.99.

I figure, easy on, easy off.

If I chicken out or change my mind, I'm only out fifteen dollars, plus tax. I add a couple pairs of thong underwear. That should get me through the audition. The girls wear big shoes, but shoes are quite an investment, easily seventy dollars for a good pair. I can't bring myself to spend that much for what may end up being a total bust. No pun intended.

Like most women I know, I do have some clothing items that feature prominently in my closet, which I have never mustered the guts to wear. For me, it is a pair of black thigh-high boots that I ordered from a catalog ages ago. If nothing else, I have now managed to come up with the appropriate venue for their debut.

I'm not ready to commit seventy bucks on stripper shoes yet. Despite my strange little fantasy and last night's daring venture into a real live strip joint, I know I'm not really a dancer. In my real life I can *pass* for a stripper, but one would not likely mistake me for one.

First of all, I'm a Jewish mother, not to mention a Jewish daughter. I'm not sure exactly what I mean by that, but when I think Jewish, I think Rhoda, and Jewish American Princesses (even though I've never actually met one), and of my four and a half foot tall grandmother. I think starchy foods, and Woody Allen, and funny words like shmuck and shlemiel, but I don't think of strippers.

Second, I do have alternative career options should exotic dancing fail to pan out for me. I've spent the last nine consecutive years of my life studying and working in a university as a research scientist and have recently completed my doctorate. At present, I carry a briefcase for a top management consulting company.

When I saw the ad for my current position, it called for knowledge of gender and race discrimination law, statistics, and programming experience, a rare collection of background and skills that I happened to possess. The job sounded very exciting and completely different than anything I had ever done. For someone just starting out, it is an incredible opportunity.

Unfortunately, with this great opportunity, I also find myself on the politically incorrect side of cases, defending large corporations accused of gender, race, or age discrimination, some, in my opinion, quite rightfully. I feel tremendously conflicted. My liberal, Jewish sensibilities notwithstanding, our consulting team is the best money can buy and I am proud to be a part of it. I remind myself that everyone is entitled to representation, but I can't say that it doesn't bother me. The line between expert and advocate is so blurry. I don't support the glass ceiling; I am a pane in it.

Finally, as far as what concerns me most about becoming a stripper, or participating in the sex industry in any capacity, is that I have always considered myself to be a feminist. I want the freedom to do with my body whatever I please, but I also know that my personal choices have political significance. My collusion with the sex trade may perpetuate and reinforce distinctions and divisions of

18

labor by gender, strengthening the boundaries that limit the collective choices available to women.

Nevertheless, I would argue that many more men than women, given the opportunity, would happily exchange renewable sexual resources for cash. This leads me to believe that it is not the commodification of sexuality that poses a dilemma, but the inequality of the exchange within the context of global economic inequalities between men and women. Despite my persistent misgivings, I believe that increased social acceptance of the sex industry would be far more beneficial to women than any attempts to eliminate the industry have ever been.

In the introduction to his book Behind the G-String, David A. Scott describes the quintessential stripper.

"She is willful, self-possessed, commanding, and most scandalously, she is unabashed about it all. There is no hint of vulnerability in her exposure before strangers. She is shameless. It is this component of the stripper's image that is the most grievous, because it signifies that she is somehow immune to social control. To be beyond shame — the internalized punishment for stepping out of line — is to be free of the need to belong."

I love it. God knows I'd never want to belong to a club that would have me as a member and the way he puts it, who wouldn't want to be her? Shameless. I say the word again out loud and it sounds too, too delicious.

Immune to social control, a state of being that I doubt most women could even begin to imagine. I've been feeling this hard to pinpoint sense of regret, highlighted by my new ill-fitting career, of something left undone. If, by my description, I seem to elevate disrobing in public to the equivalent of climbing a mountain with Sir Edmund Hillary, I apologize, but if I really wanted to climb Mt. Everest, at least I could tell my mother about it.

Every aspect of my life for the past few years has been one fear-based decision after another. I stopped looking ahead to possibilities, but saw only pitfalls to avoid. For years, I stayed in a job I hated simply to maintain my benefits, only to jump at the chance to take this

STRIPPER SHOES

job, at far less money than I deserved, out of fear that another offer
may not materialize. Maybe somewhere in my head I think stripping
is the antidote to my long streak of right choices for all the wrong
reasons - the wrong choice for the right reasons? Stripping is
something I've wanted to try, but haven't, not because I think it's
wrong or bad, but because I'm afraid. Now I have yet another fear-
based choice to make; I'm afraid of getting older and having this
giant, flashing, unchecked box on my to-do list forever.

I want to know what its like to dance up on a stage and be one of
those wild women who seem so different and separate from the rest of
us. I want to experience for myself the stripper mystique and not let
fear stop me from trying something new. I am dying to walk a mile in
their dangerous, sexy, anything but practical shoes.

Neither of my kids are at home when I get back from my shopping
trip, so I try on the outfit and practice a little of what I plan to do
when I get on stage. It doesn't seem worth spending too much time
practicing an act. Once I actually get on stage, I know I won't
remember a single thing. I'll have to rely on my basic ability to move
with the music and remember to try and look sexy. And make eye
contact.

And take my top off.

Okay, yes, I'm very nervous. I can still change my mind and not
show up tomorrow night. I can drop it. I can just forget the whole
thing and no one will even know that I was thinking about it.
Oh God, what if I fall? What if my body is ugly and no one
comes near me? What am I supposed to do up there? What if I freeze
in the spotlight? What if I make a complete fool out of myself and
people laugh at me? What if nobody tips me?

As I lie in bed, staring up at the ceiling, I can't stop thinking about
it. I tug on the loose skin around my middle and run my fingers over
the rough terrain of my stretch marks, and one more time remind
myself that the lighting is dim. Determined, I decide that - mystique
or no mystique - if some eighteen-year-old girl from Podunk Nowhere

can do it, there is no reason to think I can't do it, too. Eventually, after turning these thoughts around and around in my head at least five hundred times, I fall asleep.

The Divine Secrets of the Ta Ta Sisterhood

Move back just a little
let me watch your hips sway
hold me looser still
throw me like I'm wet clay
and you a feast I devour
if you let me be the man of the hour
cause you are rhythm I'm a cold shower
wait baby wait I'm reaching in your pocket baby wait
baby wait it's coming
wait baby wait I'm deeper in your pocket baby now
baby now it's coming
private figure skater I love when your eyes fix
up and down figure eighter
you stick with the old tricks
and you alone my soul entrancer
let me be your private dancer
cause you got moves motion me an answer
carnival hazy eyes tango lovers tranquilize
in patterned prances secret glances
of high strung tip toe fringe of a taut brown leather
strikes me down with the weight of a feather
we'll be moving love forever together

— Wait Artist: Huffamoose
CD: We've Been Had Again

Tips In: $8

My day job has been particularly stressful lately.

Competing priorities and simultaneous deadlines are taking their toll on my ordinarily mild enough temperament, as well as on my home life. I'm still fairly new to the job, and I've been having a great deal of trouble fitting in with the existing corporate culture. Maybe I'm a big baby, but the people here do not seem very nice. Every day,

23

twice a day, they have to pass by my office to get to their own, but never once do they bother to say good morning or goodnight.

I'm told that what I perceive to be poor manners is simply the culture of this work group, and I am a nuisance for questioning it. Lynne, our team manager, sat me down and explained that when she starts a new job, she does what she can to fit in and wouldn't expect others to be more like her. I guess she's right, but have you ever worked anywhere where people didn't say good morning? It's not that it's so bad, I mean, it's not like they spit in my coffee, not that I know of anyway, but I do think its strange, and at the very least, impolite. Maybe I am too sensitive.

If it is any indication, when I finally pack up my things and head for the club, I'm thrilled to imagine myself as Cheryl, the stripper, as opposed to Cheryl, the overeducated corporate punk.

I arrive at the club about forty-five minutes early and walk straight to the dressing room to fix myself up. When I get behind the dressing room curtains, I take a deep breath, more to shake off the residual tension of my workday than to quell any misgivings over what I am about to do. I'm acutely aware of my fear, but I am here, and I am determined to get up there, no matter what. The only way I can really embarrass myself now is if I walk back out to my car and drive home with this mission undone.

The counter top is cluttered with curling irons and make up bags, and I have to lean in to get some mirror space. I add eyeliner, touch up my face, and brush my hair, but other than that, I don't put on a lot of extra make up. Some of the dancers are putting on rainbow eye shadow and adding rhinestones or glitter to their faces and bodies. It looks like fun, playing dress up. Some are fabulously glamorous, with perfect nails, tanned skin and gorgeous clothes. I might try it some other time, but for now, I want to keep everything as simple as possible. There are signs posted all over the dressing room forbidding the use of lotions and oils, because the next dancer could easily slip on the residue left on the stage. I smear a little body make-up on to smooth out the stretch marks and random blemishes.

For the record, this isn't my first foray into public nudity. A few years back I signed up at my university to be a model for the art department. I have never been comfortable in my own skin, and being able to open myself up in a personal, but very neutral environment went a long way to free me from the harsh inner judge left over from my twenties.

When you are painted, you do not stand in contrast to some air brushed waif in a magazine. You stand alone, a thing of beauty. I gained a new appreciation for the human form in general and my body in particular. The act of being nude without feeling judged, rational or otherwise, strengthened my character and diluted my vanity. Similarly, I feel something richly feminine and womanly going on here in this club. Most of the dancers are hardly Playboy or Cosmo perfect, but quirky and flawed. They are sexy because of their variation from impossible standards, not despite them. They seem to embody a confidence in their personal gifts that I am eager to learn.

My big deal, grown-up career — the life I'm supposed to want, that I worked so hard and so long to get - isn't going the way I had imagined, and the memory of that little victory in front of fifteen art students is what first got me to think about trying something entirely different. I have choices; I don't have to keep going along just because I've already invested so much. I can paint over myself if I decide that I want to. All I have to do is decide that I want to.

I get dressed and go to the bar to get a drink, a strong gin and tonic. I slam it back and make my way to the DJ booth to give him the virtually unknown song I brought with me to play for my first dance, "Wait" by Huffamoose. The lyrics are sensual and suggestive, but not crude. It has a certain resonant depth and rhythm that reminds me of old-fashioned burlesque.

My husband, Allan, would be upset about me drinking. He'd say, "If you want to do this so badly, why do you need a drink to go through with it?" I don't have a good answer, so I won't mention it when I call him later. He's okay with me dancing, supportive anyway, and understanding that I didn't want him here to see me do it. If he were here, I'd be much too self-conscious. I don't want this to be a shared memory that we reminisce about in our old age. I did promise to call him as soon as I get off stage and before I leave the club so that he doesn't worry.

25

STRIPPER SHOES

The DJ, Marcus, must weigh about three hundred pounds and has a fantastic smile. He seems very friendly and genuinely willing to help me. Typically, I wouldn't give friendliness a second thought, but I guess I've become a little skittish about people lately, and I'm not sure what to expect here. I tell him my new fake name and he says he'll let me know when it's my turn. I give him the CD and tell him it's the first song.

"Okay, Trinity, the stage back there is Stage Two, on this wall here is Stage Three. Nearest to me is Stage One and back in the smoking lounge is Stage Four. When I call you, you'll go to Stage One. You have to get on the stage before the dancer you follow can leave, you understand?"

"Yes, she can't go until I get up there."

"Right, and these are three song sets, you always take your top off during the second song. You want me to play the song you brought first or second?" I don't really understand what he's asking me, it's loud in the booth and I'm nervous, but I say to play it first. This meant that I would have my big moment to some other song and use the one I brought to coax me into it.

I'm glad to be feeling the effects of the gin, because it'll be my turn after two more sets. Marcus asks me what kind of music I like. Like me, he is a few years older than most of the strippers and other DJs in here and we bond over our preference for classic rock. I want to hang around in the booth with him, but I vaguely recall this activity to be among the many prohibitions. Instead, I sit down not far from him and watch the succession of dancers until my new stage name is called.

It seems like a painfully long wait, but soon it's my turn. This is it. I have to go up there and not make a complete fool out of myself. That is truly my one concern now that it's all about to happen - looking stupid. I don't care if I look naked, I just don't want to look like a moron.

I'm following a beautiful blonde. She's a tall, voluptuous girl. Curvaceous and extremely beautiful, with gorgeous, enormous, quite obviously natural breasts. Marcus announces that Trinity is next up, "Trinity's first time anywhere! Get yourself to Stage One and take good care of her!"

26

Melanie offers her hand and welcomes me up onto the stage as she gathers her dollar bills and clothes. I pace slowly and don't focus my eyes on anything in particular until I hear my song go into full swing. I start moving around, using up every square foot of the stage. I'm tipsy enough to feel relaxed, but not so much that I'm worried about falling. I concentrate on how much I like the song and keep dancing to enjoy myself. I'm not nervous. Now that I've started, and I'm moving around up here, the only thing I could do now that would embarrass me would be to chicken out. Even if I trip or struggle with my outfit, as long as I do what I came here to do, I'll leave feeling satisfied.

Several men are seated around the stage and a few have dollar bills out in front of them. I was told and shown how to take the dollar bills. I hike the hem of my dress up as I dance until they can see my thong underpants. For the customers with their money out, I kneel or lean down and stretch the side of my thong out at my hip for them to put the money in. The men seem to know the drill even if I don't. They are not allowed to actually touch me so they take the bills, fold them lengthwise and place them inside the edge of my panty. I let the thong snap back on the money for dramatic effect.

My body is moving with no regard to conscious choice. My brain must really be frozen or hiding in shame because normally it would never allow such blatant insubordination. I'm still nervous that I'll screw up and get into trouble, do something I'm not supposed to do, forget to do something I am supposed to do.

Somehow, completely brain-free, I keep dancing and taking money. I focus on the music, and if I let any thought at all cross my mind, it's the repetition of one phrase, "Keep moving."

Before I know it, we're on the second song. I look over at another stage and see the dancer removing her top, so I slide the straps of my cheap outfit over my shoulders and pull the front down. It's that simple. All I have on while I dance are my big boots, my thong, and the sheath of checkered lycra dress bunched up around my middle.

More money makes its way to the stage when the top comes off. This convention becomes immediately apparent. They want you to come closer in order to grab the money after you have removed your top and don't want to waste their allotment of bills for the night while your top is still on. Even in my brain-free state, I get it.

27

On the third song, as I dance and take more dollar bills, I get the dress completely off. By this time it doesn't even feel like that big of a deal. The first few seconds of pulling it off and exposing my breasts is creepy, but once that is over, I only feel silly. I still grab whatever money is to be had, but I do feel ridiculous. Whatever ingrained taboo I was expecting to lift from my psyche, did, in fact, disappear, but strikingly unceremoniously.

There aren't many men at my stage, and all of them are cheap. When I get off the stage and count, I had made a pathetic eight dollars. Eight bucks. Cheryl, you just danced around with your tits hanging out for the whole world to see for eight bucks.

I don't care. I did it. I didn't let fear or negative soundtracks that play in my head get in my way, and I can't take it back now even if I wanted to. I scurry to the dressing room to pull myself together. The girls congratulate me and ask me how much I made, and I go back out to see if I got the job. I meet with Michael, the owner, in his office.

Michael is a personable, nice looking immigrant from the Middle East, who I would guess to be between forty and fifty years old. He says I looked good out there. Does anyone ever look bad out there?

He asks me how many days I want to work. I explain about my day job and Michael is very flexible about it, providing me with three different contact phone numbers should there ever be a problem. Although I don't give him specifics regarding my qualifications, he seems impressed with my work ethic and mentions that he has a master's degree in engineering. He gives me a schedule of Monday, Tuesday and Friday nights, 8:00 to 2:00, and Saturdays, 2:00 to 8:00 PM; fewer shifts than Kurt said I would have to work, so I'm happy.

I ask if I can start tonight, but he has too many dancers on the floor already. He says I can try to pick up a table dance if I want to. Michael sends me back to the DJ booth to tell Marcus my schedule. Marcus also congratulates me on my first performance and blames the low rate of return on the fact that it is still very early. I'm being patted on the back for a nice strip show, but the overall weirdness of this does not sink in, I'm too busy being relieved, proud of myself, and trying to figure out what I want to do before I go home for the night.

I sit at Stage Two and watch other women dance. Later, I find out that this is only acceptable as long as you are moving money out of the patron's pockets and onto the stage. Next to me is a good looking young man named Ryan. He is of average height, nice build, fair skinned with very short, razor-shorn hair and intense blue-gray eyes. Trying to be funny, I ask him if he is a skinhead.

He is not amused. However, we start talking and I tell him that this is my first night, my audition, and my first time ever. He thinks I'm making it up, that I've really done this before but my ignorance and naïveté surface quickly. Eventually he believes me and enthusiastically offers advice. He leaves a customary two dollars on the stage so he can keep talking to me without the dancer onstage glaring at him or taking it out on me later. He is the first, but certainly not the last to make me aware of this convention.

I see Ryan as a great way to start learning about what goes on here. He's a regular of sorts and I can't help but ask the obvious question right away, "You seem pretty normal to me, I'm sure you could get a real girl if you tried. What the heck are you doing here?"

"I never have the chance to meet anyone." He works as an intern in a nursing home, enjoys it, but doesn't meet a lot of women, at least not those his own age. I don't know who he expects to meet hanging around in here. I think he should be spending his evenings looking for a nice girl and settle down. He likes strip clubs, and he hasn't much more to say about it. Ryan doesn't want to talk about himself for long. I can tell he much prefers the idea of coaching me in the art of striptease.

"The key is to look into their eyes. Make them believe you want them. Make them believe that you could be their girlfriend someday. Look deep into their eyes. Stare into a guy's eyes like you want him. Some girls avoid eye contact; you can see they hate it. The guys who come in here want to feel a connection, they don't want to pay to feel rejected. You can understand that, can't you?"

I am to find this last piece of advice to be only partially true. Some men love the chase and initial rejection as part of the fulfillment of their extended fantasy, but for the most part, Ryan proves to understand the system of exchange extremely well.

We talk for a while and I start thinking about my first table dance. I'm on a roll, and I want to get it over with. I ask him if he'd like a table dance and although I can sense he is reluctant, I push because I want my first one to be with someone with whom I feel comfortable and who would also be willing to give me suggestions. It doesn't hurt that he is also young and attractive. I say I'll do it for free if he tells me what to do, that way I won't embarrass myself with my first paying customer.

When a person has never before seen a private dance performed, it's the getting started part that is the problem. Normally it is twenty dollars for one song. By now I'm starting on my third drink, which Ryan paid for, but technically I didn't solicit, and I am determined to go through with this. We walk to the long, narrow mirrored stage area that is alongside and to the right of the DJ booth. Customers sit in chairs facing the mirror and dancers sit or stand on the stage. We can touch them as long as our clothes are still on, so I don't immediately remove anything and wait for him to instruct me as to appropriate table dance protocol.

I sit on the floor with my back to the mirrored wall, and I try to engage him with my eyes as I pose in front of him. I keep my eyes fixed on him and put my hands on his shoulders and rub them with an abrupt determination. I throw in a little of what I have seen before and flip my hair over, letting it drag down to his lap. I'm not sure why the hair thing is supposed to be sexy, but I am positive that I've seen it before. I try hard to be sensual and not appear to be self-conscious and hyper-aware of my own behavior, even though I am visibly shaking from nerves.

The more I try to hide it, the worse I get. I don't entirely get over the awkward nature of the situation, but I try my hardest to focus on the moment instead of thinking about how I will describe the scene later. Focus eludes me, but my anxiety subsides. I have a very low tolerance for alcohol, and finally after the adrenaline rush that killed my initial buzz, I am at least a little drunk. Ryan reminds me again to keep my gaze on him.

I expected to be grossed out by doing a private dance, but Ryan is good looking, a solid ten years younger than I am, and in the real world would probably not give me a second look. It doesn't feel that terrible and again, I don't feel dirty. My test case is achieving an obvious erection watching me, and I am strangely proud of myself. I like the feeling of power and the validation that I am sexually attractive to him, and I wonder if the other dancers enjoy a sense of victory or accomplishment, or if it's a non-issue. I don't know why I care whether I give some random guy a hard-on, but I do.

I feel confident enough to pull down my top and keep going. I suck in my stomach and do a variety of foolish-looking and embarrassing moves, mostly simulating masturbation, while at the same time trying not to break any rules. I use my upper arms to squeeze my breasts together and run my hands on my thighs and above my groin area, without actually touching myself. From his angle it looks fairly authentic.

With my backside to him, I think of yoga poses I could have learned, but didn't. I arch my back as deeply as I can and linger watching his face in the mirror directly in front of me. Then I turn and sit facing him, spread my legs and get up on my knees to kneel close enough to him to stare into his eyes again.

Regardless of what position I end up in, he remains steadfastly focused on my eyes. I can feel myself becoming aroused as he stares so intently at me with his piercing gaze. I'm enjoying this too much, feeling him want me. It's been twenty years since I've felt so excited and yet completely unable to do anything about it. Like being fifteen with a high school sweetheart in my parent's basement, except with bouncers standing by.

I can't figure out why I am supposed to think this is bad. If I weren't married, well, if I weren't me, I'd be getting directions to this guy's apartment instead of having him teach me to earn tips by suggesting, and then refusing, what could potentially be fabulous sex. For that matter, since when does any Jewish girl need lessons in the art of withholding sex for fun and profit? The things we figure out when it's too damn late.

When at least two songs have gone by, while we're only supposed to do one or be paid for more, I've done everything I can think of doing. I stop and ask him what he thought. He stammers, "Good. It was great, thank you," and tries to give me the twenty even though I said it was free. I don't accept it, though I suppose a real stripper would have, and thank him for his advice.

I have to get up for work tomorrow. I'm ready to go home and my body language must make it evident, because Ryan walks away from me and finds a seat at one of the stages. Michael calls me back into his office and he kindly, but firmly informs me that they are paying twenty dollars for one song, so be sure to take my top off right away. I reply that I understand, and I will be sure to do that the next time.

"Did he pay you?" He wants to make sure I wasn't stiffed. I realize now how much they watch everything, and I make a mental note of it.

"I offered to do it for free in exchange for his advice on my first time." I can tell that Michael isn't thrilled by the freebie and isn't quite sure what to make of me, but he gives me a nod and lets it go. I feel stupid, I should have taken the money or lied about it to Michael, but I am a lousy liar, and sometimes I don't think on my feet all that well. I shrug it off and make the long drive home, proud of my accomplishment and looking forward to my first night as an exotic dancer.

What Do They Know About
The Classics?

It is better to have a permanent income than to be fascinating.
— Oscar Wilde

Take home: $125
Tipped out: $30

I had a typical lousy day at work.

The women here hate me. I used to think they hated me in particular, but it turns out that they pretty much treat everyone like crap, not just me. This makes me feel a little better, but it doesn't make the days any more pleasant. For the most part, I sit around in my office hoping they'll forget I exist. Sometimes they do. Those are the good days, but this wasn't one of them.

We had to work on a project cooped up in a room together and it looks like this project could go on for weeks. The truth is, I couldn't be more different from them, and when I'm forced to be near them I end up trying much too hard to be liked. So I try to make small talk or jokes, but all I get are blank stares like I'm from another planet. I get nervous and say things that are even more stupid and/or offensive than I would under normal circumstances. A few days ago I got into a little trouble. We had another long day ahead of us, and I made the mistake of starting it off with the following comment, "Look, I'm about to get my period, so if I burst into tears, I just want you all to know it has nothing to do with any of you." True, I lack some sense of propriety, but I swear to God I have never worked with a group of women who wouldn't bond over period chatter. As long as there are no men around, all the women I've ever known are completely comfortable with stuff like that.

They freaked. Like I had just hopped up on the conference table and taken a big poop — that was how they looked at me. And it wasn't enough to let me feel stupid about it and move on, I had to be dressed down about "fitting into the existing culture" again later that day.

33

So today it was getting to be about six o'clock, and it was clear that we were going to have to stay even later, but I wanted to be out the door with plenty of time to mentally prepare myself for my new job. Conscientious as I typically am, I let Lynne know ahead of time that I needed to leave no later than 7:30.

She said, "Well I really need you to stay as long as it takes tonight, (in her phony, sickly-sweet, power-hungry, sucking-all-the-joy-from-every-minute way) but if you absolutely need to go then I guess you need to go." When all was said and done, the others decided to go home about 6:30, and I ended up taking that additional crap from Lynne for nothing.

I took what Delilah said to heart and bought a bag and a lock to take with me and store my clothes. I packed it with some thongs and three reasonably convincing stripper outfits. One was the stretchy dress that I bought at Fascinations and wore on my audition. I also found a black vinyl-but-looks-like-leather outfit that has buckles on it, and finally a tube dress that would normally be used as a slip. I've got my big boots and a couple pairs of high-heeled shoes.

I get to the club a little early and after dressing, I go to the DJ booth to give him my CD. It's Marcus again, and he seems genuinely happy to see me. We talk for a while about our other jobs and our kids. He is a filmmaker (independent films, not pornography as I might have assumed) and has a daughter that he clearly adores. Marcus reminds me one more time of how the rotations work.

He puts a dance list on a message board behind him that we follow unless he calls us up over the PA system to let us know that he's modified it. The key is to remember which dancer you follow and pay attention to where she is. For the most part, dancers move from stage to stage in consecutive order, but one doesn't necessarily start on Stage One, and depending on how many dancers there are, there can be quite a bit of time between each dancer's set. Plus the number of songs per set varies. One can use the time in between to change, talk to men, relax in the dressing room, or, most preferably, get table dances. Talking to men and letting them buy you drinks makes money for the club, and certainly helps one develop regulars, but table dances are twenty dollars a song, so that's how the dancers make the bulk of their take-home pay.

I introduce myself to Paul the bartender and buy myself a drink at an outrageous price even with our employee discount. I explain to Paul that under no circumstances should I ever be served more than two drinks in one night. I get drunk so fast that if I were to engage in a third, I can't be held responsible for my behaviors. He says it's no problem. If men want to buy me drinks later in the evening after drink number two, that I should order something clear and he'll fill my glass with 7-Up.

I sit down at a table with some men until its time for the shift change. During the shift change, both night and day shift dancers get up on the stages, so there are four or five women on each stage at least, and we stretch, cool down and talk to each other and to customers sitting around the stages. They call it "The Zoot Scoot". The purpose is to signal that it's time to get started, or get going, and it also gives the DJ the chance to see who is working the next shift and make the dance list.

The DJ reminds the customers that day shift dancers are leaving so if there is one special girl they want to get a table dance from, they'd better hurry. Even though I understand the function of this process, it gets under my skin. We are on display for the customers to look us over all at once and I find it particularly demeaning. Maybe I feel more uncomfortable about this particular job requirement as compared to some other potentially more distasteful ones because it is the only one I can't control. We have to get up there, stay on stage as long as it takes, they play this boring house music the whole time, and we're really not dancing or making money, we're just on display. I don't like it.

While I'm stretching and spreading my legs and moving around in various unnatural poses, another dancer gets my attention with an urgent expression. She tells me that she can see right through my thong and that I'd better go change before Michael hears about it. This was a pair I had lying around in a drawer and until now I hadn't noticed. I hop off the stage and dig up a new pair as fast as I can. We aren't supposed to leave the stage, but I bolt to the dressing room to change into another thong and come right back.

Thanking her profusely for helping me stay out of trouble, she smiles and waves it off. I get no sense that she is trying to be a jerk or boss me around. She knew I didn't know any better and was doing

35

me a favor. She could have minded her own business and let me get into all kinds of trouble, but she didn't. Besides the bonus exposure at no additional charge, no harm was done, and I was already very impressed with the supportive atmosphere.

I expected strippers to be competitive and catty. On the contrary, I can't remember having seen as much friendliness and teamwork in any other job I've had. In contrast, a frequent topic of discussion is Tinseltown, a club south of here, considered to be one of the premier strips club in the area. The customer traffic is higher and the dancers take home pay is fabled to be substantially greater, however, the dancers are said to be intensely competitive and treacherous. It is universally agreed by Allure's dancers in-the-know, that such an atmosphere of "every girl for herself" is not worth the extra cash.

When the house music ends and the first two dancers are called on stage, I check the dance list. I'm to start on Stage Two, which means I won't get to pick the music. Whoever is on Stage One gets her music played, and eventually it will be my turn again. Marcus plays the choice of the woman on Stage One, the ubiquitous hip-hop urban youth dance music. Although it is not my favorite, I have no problem getting into the music and dancing. This time it is a piece of cake. It's Friday and unlike my audition, the stage is already almost completely surrounded. I like the feeling of the tension in my arms as I swing myself around the poles and the way it feels to perform in front of an audience.

Even if the customers don't care how well I dance, I do.

My eyes keep returning to the big brass poles. I stare at them longingly, but not in an absurd, Freudian, phallic way. I wish I could use them in my performance like some of the other dancers do. They pull themselves up and spin around or flip upside down and slowly slide down. They look so cool on those poles. For now, I use them to lean against or swing myself around, but I want to learn to do something more gymnastic and flashy someday.

I lean over and kneel on the stage and pick up dollar bills in the side of my T-bar with absolutely no shame. Shameless. I smile and enjoy myself. I don't know how I look up here, but I'm not self-conscious, and it feels good. The customers can tell I'm having a good time, and they are responding positively towards me. They want to connect with this girl they've never seen before who is having so much fun on stage. By the second song, I remind myself that I need to stare into different guys eyes and make them think I want them.

One thing that became clear to me during my brief stint as a stripper, and I can't emphasize this enough, is that men love tits. As much as we think they love tits, they love them even more than that. And they like to see as many different sets of them as possible. There are many complex reasons that strip clubs endure, but sometimes the simplest explanation can be the most useful. It's nothing personal. It also doesn't really matter if I'm not the best looking girl, or have the best body, or the best dancer or even in the top twenty on any of these measures. Men are always happy to see tits and never seem to get tired of it. Huggy Bear probably could have taught me that too, if it weren't for the network censors.

An elderly gentleman starts talking to me and I can barely hear or understand him. I must have spent too much time trying, because later Michael called me into his office and told me not to talk so long to anyone while I'm on stage. It's still early in the evening and we are doing three song sets, much too long, but when I'm done, I bend over in an exaggerated manner trying to be funny and gather up my dollar bills as the next dancer steps up. If I hurry to put my money away and get back out there, I'm pretty sure I can get at least one of these guys to buy a table dance.

When I get into the dressing room, I can't open the lock on my bag. I'm pulling and tugging and swearing, but I think it is bent. I'm already very nervous about doing a good job and I start to panic that I won't be able to change in time for my next set. While I've been struggling with my lock, it seems that the DJ has been calling me over the PA, "Trinity, come to the DJ booth, Trinity to the DJ booth."

First of all, I don't hear him; second, I'm not sure that I would have remembered that I am supposed to be Trinity. I'm too busy freaking that I can't get my bag open. Michael knocks on the dressing room door and someone signals that it is clear for him to come in. Apparently he can see us topless out on stage, but not in the dressing room.

"Trinity, the DJ has called you three times, get out there!"

"Umm, I'm having a problem…I'm having a problem, my bag won't open… I can't get the lock open." Oh God, I am such a dweeb. Michael says he'll send someone in with a tool to cut the lock and I attempt to regain some composure. I go to see the DJ and tell him that I am a bit hard of hearing. If he needs me he's going to have to be especially loud when he calls "Trinity." He reminds me to relax and take it easy, it's no problem, and he just wanted to let me know that I'd be following a different dancer for the rest of the night. I explain that I am locked out of my bag, and he offers to give me plenty of time before my next set.

Rick, a bouncer, shows up just a few minutes later with bolt cutters. I meet him for the first time as he shyly enters the forbidden zone dressing room and proceeds to cut the lock off my bag. He is about 6'4," very muscular and at least thirty-five, maybe forty plus, a sweet combination of steroids and sincerity. He introduces himself by vigorously shaking my hand and giving me the rundown of who he is and what he does. Rick has done this line of work for years and takes great pride in protecting us. He lets me know for the first of many times that if I need any help, if anyone gets out of line, any problem whatsoever, he is strip-club-bouncer-Johnny-on-the-spot and don't hesitate to let him know.

The doormen, all of the bouncers, the DJ, and the bartenders have what appears to me to be a fairly elaborate communication system using earpieces and microphones. Also, there are cameras all over the place. I feel reasonably safe already, but Rick is dying to kick somebody's ass in defense of one of the dancers. This is particularly amusing to me because from what I can tell so far, the clientele is almost exclusively made up of white-collar middle managers and IT professionals. It's the thought that counts, and I can't help but like him. The lock is off, and I'm good to go.

Because it's Friday, there are many dancers on tonight, so I only get to dance a few more sets. I sit and talk to a lot of men and I offer table dances, but it has already been such a stressful night that I don't push it. I'll try harder next time. I move through a rotation until I finally get back to Stage One where I get to pick the tunes. This time, instead of choosing specific songs, I ask Marcus to play some random disco. When I get on stage and hear the intro to "It's Raining Men", all the stress I felt earlier in the dressing room breaks loose and I crack up laughing. He follows it up with "I Will Survive", another disco staple. I am surprised to find out how difficult it is to strip to these songs. When I return to the dressing room, some of the dancers playfully boo and hiss my play list. What do they know about the classics?

At the end of the night, we all have to get up on stage again as they clear the customers out. When they are gone, we file back into the dressing room, which is as crowded as it ever gets. It's claustrophobic, and I have trouble pulling all my junk back together and into my now unprotected bag.

I'm hurrying to get out of there because I don't remember that we are not free to go just as soon as we are ready. Yet another element of the job that sticks in my craw: We have to wait for all the customers to be gone, return all our dishes and glasses to the bar, and clean up the back before we are even allowed to exit the dressing room, much less leave the club. Once that is done, we can wait out in the club for the parking lot to be cleared of all customers. I'm tired and cranky and it seems to take forever.

Girls are strewn all over the place, exhausted and draped over chairs, smoking and counting from their piles of money. They've washed their faces and are back in their street clothes, baggy sweats, and thick, out of fashion eyeglasses. Some of them look downright homely. The glamorous, young woman who sent me running to the dressing room to change my see-through thong, now looks like any woman you'd never notice on the bus.

We need to tip everybody out. That means the DJ, the bar, the doormen and bouncers. Tonight this means six people at a respectable minimum of five dollars each. I can see that some dancers tip less, but then you hear a lot of under-the-breath complaining, and promises not to look after that girl quite as diligently. I see no interest in alienating anyone, or feeling less protected, so I tip out generously, with the additional motive of getting the male personnel to like me and hopefully talk freely with me whenever the opportunity arises.

All night I have been stuffing bills into my bag. I pull out enough to give everyone five dollars each, but I don't want to count it while

39

I'm still in the club, I just want to go home. Finally, the guys say its clear, and they walk us to our cars and watch to see that we get out safely.

It's a long drive home, and I get in around 3:00 AM. I'm tired all the way down to my bones, but I can't wait until morning. I hop into bed to count the money from my very first night as an exotic dancer. I unzip the flap on the bag where I've been stuffing my tips and let it all fall out into a pile. They are mostly ones so it makes a pretty big pile. Then I notice it.

An ugly stench quickly fills up the room and our nostrils.
The money stinks.

Not the typical smoky bar smell. Years ago, Allan played drums in numerous nightclub bands and his musical equipment still carries that smell. This is different. It's unique, and it permeates every dollar. Men have laid out these dollars, put them in their pockets, folded and unfolded them in their hands, fingered them anxiously, and then placed them next to my skin. There is a sickly sweetness to it. The closest I can come to describing it is by comparing it to the animal odor that is exuded when dogs fight.

It's probably just the combination of leather wallet, smoky bar, and stripper sweat. Allan jokes that this tainted income is the harbinger of evil forces, an ironic premise of a Stephen King novel. I laugh, but inside it really gets to me.

I can label the stench — it smells desperate.

I start to feel like maybe I'm doing something very wrong, but I put my superstitions and worries aside for the time being.

Smell or no smell, it won't stop me from spending it.

Please, No Lectures

If A is success in life, then A equals x plus y plus z.
Work is x; y is play; and z is keeping your mouth shut.

— *Albert Einstein*

We're still working pointlessly on case files for "as long as it takes". I'd much rather take the work back to my own office, but we need to stay in the room together so we can do spot checks now and then to ensure consistency among our ratings. Week after week it's one petty little indignity after another. Silly things, that for some reason, I do not seem to have the wherewithal to rise above.

My very first day here, Lynne, Mary Beth, and Jane invited me to lunch. Then they changed their minds, but apparently forgot to tell me. Around two in the afternoon, I saw Jane and asked what time we were leaving. She explained that they had gone their separate ways and already had lunch. No apology, in fact, only Jane even acknowledged that I had been left behind, and that was only because I asked. Things only got worse from there.

When I first started in this job, about two weeks into my training period, Lynne and I got into an argument over email. It was more of a miscommunication than an argument; one of many early signs that I had made a huge mistake. During our exchange, I felt put down and lectured to and in my email response to Lynne I wrote, "Please, no lectures."

Afterwards, I thought we had talked it all out and gone past it. I didn't think about it again until this morning when I joined them in the conference room. I don't know what they were originally joking about, but Mary Beth leaned over to Lynne, and in a mocking, exaggerated tone said, "Please, no lectures!"

I can only assume that they have made fun of it so many times since it happened that Mary Beth has forgotten where it originated. My heart went up into my throat, but I pretended that I didn't hear her. I went to the ladies room and sat in the stall for a while with my face in my hands. Weeping is a fairly common activity in the restroom of this firm, but I couldn't let myself cry because I knew I had to go back in there and get back to business.

My friends were so happy and excited for me when I took this job, I don't want to tell them how badly it's going. I can't imagine what I'd say or how I would explain what's been going on with me over the last few months. I don't want them to know how poorly I've been handling all these changes or that nobody here likes me. It's sounds so ridiculous. Every day normal people take normal jobs and handle the normal bumps in the road just fine.

I wonder what my friends will think if I tell them what I've been up to. I worry that they will speculate about my motivations in very unflattering directions. They might say that I'm silly and insecure and desperate for attention, and maybe they are right. Maybe they will think that I am experiencing a mid-life crisis and nothing I try to explain to them after that will be taken seriously. I'll be patronized. I'm petrified of what they'll think and that is why I don't tell them.

I'm afraid to tell them that I'm working as a stripper, and that I want to write about it, because they will have every reason to be amused by my foolishness. If I tell them and they think less of me for it, then I'll be risking my friends right along with my career. I'm just not that sure about any of this, so for now, I'll keep it to myself.

Breathe. Breathe Again. I want to go home.

Don't You Boys Know Any Nice Songs?

"...I know it when I see it."

— Supreme Court Justice Potter Stewart, 1964

Tips In: $138
Tips Out: $25
Spent: $20 (for shoes I bought from another dancer)

It's Saturday and I don't have to be at the club until 2:00 today. If feels great to make a real breakfast for my kids. I don't think I used the stove in the apartment once before they got here. If I didn't have to go into the office, I spent my weekend mornings eating leftover microwave popcorn and reading the newspaper.

Back home, my kids usually had friends spend the night. Weekend mornings meant stepping over sleeping teenagers, curled up in blankets on the living room floor, to get to the kitchen. I'd wake them all up with the smell of scrambled eggs and burned tofu bacon. After breakfast my son would sit on the couch and play his guitar, and his friends, one by one, would hand me their dirty dishes and compliment my scrambled eggs before going off to watch TV or play video games. Even now that they are here with me, I think about the way weekends used to be all the time.

The kids eat their breakfast then retreat back to their rooms. Allan is reading the paper. I leave for the club early so I have a chance to get dressed at a leisurely pace and talk to the other dancers. There is a particular weirdness to seeing so many pairs of boobs up on a stage in the middle of the day, in broad daylight — well, daylight if we had any windows. There are hardly any customers, plus neither the owner nor the manager is around during the day shift, so there is a much more fun, casual atmosphere.

The bad news, from my point of view anyway, is that the DJ will play music that Michael wouldn't allow if he were in — an abundance of Prince and the especially vulgar hip hop songs that these girls seem to love. Ugh. Imagine listening to "Pussy Control" over and over again. And some other song that goes "You better lick it, before we kick it, you gotta get it soft and wet before we…something, something". Thankfully, this tender ditty has yet to be committed into my long-term memory. I'm hardly Tipper Gore, it doesn't embarrass me, but this music bugs the heck out of me — yet another reminder of which side of the generation gap on which I'm beginning to fall.

The biggest fan of the filthiest songs is Pandora, a 21-year-old, fair-skinned redhead. The reason I know she is twenty-one is that she is allowed to order alcoholic beverages, and does so with great frequency.

Pandora is very outgoing and seems to want to hang out with me. I'm thrilled because even though every one has been nice to me and willing to offer help and advice, she is the first to make me feel like she wants to be friends and talk about something other than the nuts and bolts of what I need to be doing. She loves to tell me about all the sex she is having. Pandora has girlfriends, boyfriends, whatever. I don't know when she has time to sleep. She is, hands down, the horniest person I have ever met.

Not everyone is crazy about Pandora, but I find her harmless and amusing. The other night Pandora was back in the smoking lounge hanging all over a couple (yes, a couple) she had apparently been intimate with earlier that day. Meanwhile, in the dressing room, Delilah expressed her disgust at Pandora's behaviors and spread the gospel of her general disdain for lazy, slutty strippers.

"Don't you people have any goals?" she ranted to no one in particular. The few girls who couldn't ignore her piped up with good humored mocking about their immediate goals of making some big bucks tonight. This is when I learned that Delilah had just picked up a day job as a pre-school teacher and was understandably very proud of her legitimate, un-lazy, un-slutty, un-stripper activities. Because of her new day job, she would be working fewer shifts from now on and relates this information to us in a way that let me know that a) some of the dancers might resent this special treatment, and b) Delilah enjoys this potential jealousy. It occurs to me that while I am playing at being a stripper, Delilah is testing the waters of being an upstanding citizen, or at least a regular person.

I mention that when I was right about her age, I was a pre-school teacher of two-year olds. She acknowledges my interjection without comment and continues to lecture us pointlessly until she is finished putting tiny barrettes in her hair, exiting the dressing room with an air of self-satisfaction mixed with exasperation. Boot slamming would prove to be especially frequent and loud on this particular evening.

Pandora offers to share her locker with me since her previous locker-mate has since bailed, but left most of her stuff. Dancers disappear without notice on a regular basis. Often the locker-mate sells what is left behind to other dancers. Several dancers have come and gone since I started, but I'm too new to miss people or recognize which faces are new. Pandora manages to get me to buy a pair of shoes from her and let her borrow one of my favorite outfits. She's a tad manipulative and is clearly someone people rarely say no to, but I like her and despite Delilah's admonitions, I appreciate having someone to talk to.

There aren't many customers, but there aren't many dancers on either. The DJ opens up only one stage for a while, and when it's Pandora's turn, no one is sitting at her stage. I take it upon myself to round up as many men standing around the bar as I can and nag them into sitting at my new friend's stage.

Pandora doesn't really dance when she is on stage; she more or less gets into sexual poses and jiggles around with a big shit-eating grin on her face. She revels in the dirty lyrics and sings along while she lies on her back with her legs spread or on her knees with her back arched, butt in the air, shaking it around. She smacks her lips and stares at every man as though she might hop off the stage and land in his lap at any moment. If they don't like it, they ought to. She would make a lot more money, but when not on stage, she sits around the smoking lounge chattering on (if not about sex, then about being broke) instead of soliciting private dances.

Lydia, a beautiful girl about nineteen, with the longest legs I've ever seen, appears to have perfected the practice of hanging around between sets, smoking and not making any money. She's a girl-next-door type, young and fresh-faced. She has a roommate, who could easily pass as her sister, who calls herself Baby. The two of them frequently work the same shifts. They pass the time between sets together or with guys they know from outside of the club, ignoring

45

paying customers, and hence avoiding nearly every opportunity to make any real money.

Lydia is very thin, not sickly, but quite slender and is always famished when she comes in for her shift. We serve fried foods here, things like cheese sticks, pizza, chicken fingers, but she doesn't bring any money to work with her and the menu items are not cheap. I can't stand the thought of her hungry so I usually order us some to share and then make myself busy until she's finished most of it.

I listen to her boyfriend problems, she is dating one of the bouncers (a no-no that I once inadvertently let slip out), and her routine complaints about not having any money and not being able to find stage pants that are long enough to fit her. She tells me about the clubs she goes to after work. I enjoy hearing about what it's like to be that free and unencumbered by any pressing responsibilities.

I do worry about her, she seems so young and sweet to be doing this kind of thing, but this isn't even the first club she has worked in. Since I've been working long hours in both jobs, I've been missing my own kids terribly. Lydia seems to appreciate the maternal attention I give to her, and I feel less guilty about being out of the house and away from my own children so much when I know that I'm sending the extra attention her way.

Dancer Discounts and Other Perks of the Sex Industry

I once met a man with a sense of adventure
He was dressed to thrill wherever he went
He said "Let's make love on a mountain top
Under the stars on a big hard rock"
I said "In these shoes?
I don't think so"
I said "Honey, let's do it here."
So I'm sitting at a bar in Guadalajara
In walks a guy with a faraway look in his eyes
He said "I've got a powerful horse outside
Climb on the back, I'll take you for a ride
I know a little place, we can get there for the break of day."
I said "In these shoes?
No way, Jose"
I said "Honey, let's stay right here."
No le gusta caminar. No puede montar a caballo
(I don't like to walk, I can't ride a horse)
Como se puede bailar? Es un escandolo
(How can I dance? It's a scandal)
Then I met an Englishman
"Oh" he said
"Won't you walk up and down my spine,
It makes me feel strangely alive."
I said "In these shoes?
I doubt you'd survive."
I said "Honey, let's do it.
Let's stay right here."

> — *In these shoes? Artists: Kirsty MacColl &*
> *Pete Glenister CD: Tropical Brainstorm*

STRIPPER SHOES

Costumes: $338.61
   — 10% dancer discount (33.86)
   — total, plus tax: $327

I go downtown to shop for more stripper clothes. The store is upscale and the clothes are high quality. Not all the merchandise is necessarily stripper stuff, they have fancy lingerie and evening gowns, but with a certain edge to them, not like the matronly gowns that I sold when I worked in a bridal shop years ago. I tell the saleswoman that I had just started stripping, and she congratulates me excitedly and reminds me that dancers get a ten percent discount off everything in the store. She grabs about fifteen different outfits and puts me in a dressing room.

A couple outfits are just a little too deviant for my taste. I can go my whole life without a skin-tight nurse's uniform fully equipped with rubber gloves. Most of the rest of the outfits are simply unflattering. However, I did manage to find an elegant halter pantsuit that I love. It requires about two feet of hemming, but I convince myself that I might wear it out some night. I also buy some stretchy bell-bottom pants, a sequined tube top, a couple of mini-skirts, a white ruffled blouse and a short red tartan skirt to go with it. Later, I find out that Michael prefers we don't do the schoolgirl look and I end up dumping the skirt and wearing the top with other separates.

Now that I am officially a stripper, if only part-time, I bite the bullet and finally buy some stripper shoes, shiny, red, open-toe platform shoes with spike heels.

Power shoes.
Were I so inclined, I could mortally wound with these shoes.
They don't say, "Come fuck me," they say, "Go fuck yourself."

I go a little overboard with the shopping, but I treat it like an evening out and make a point of saving the receipt to write the clothes off my taxes as a business expense. Realistically, I'm not likely to make enough money for the receipt to be useful, but I keep it along with my pay stubs and a copy of the list of rules that I swiped, copied, and returned to their place of honor, tacked up in the DJ booth.

48

When I arrive at the club, I have a lot of new outfits to show off, and I feel much more glamorous and authentic. The girls are interested in my purchases and I get plenty of oohs and ahhs as I pull each item out of my bag. Then, as I should have known would happen, everyone wants to borrow from it. Annabel helps me out by gently reminding the rest of the girls that I just got all this stuff, and I should at least be able to wear it once before they all start grabbing at it.

Annabel is married and has a two-year old daughter. She looks almost exactly like Barbie would, if Barbie spent too much time in a tanning booth — very blonde and a little waxy. She is roughly 5'5" and has what I consider to be a perfect centerfold body. 34-22-34, her breasts are a perfect C cup, augmented, but not obviously so. Annabel's costumes consist mostly of evening gowns, and she is the girl most likely to be requested for a bachelor or birthday dance. When brunette dancers complain that the blondes are getting all the tips, they are actually referring to Annabel, but wouldn't want to single her out because she is much too nice to hate.

She is both beautiful and sweet. Compared to most of the rest of us, she is wholesome and has fairly decent social skills. Not that we're all crude and awful, but she is optimistic and has particularly good manners. I could easily imagine her striking up pleasant conversations while waiting in line at a grocery store. She is friendly and positive, always asking how everyone's days off were.

She tells us about being out with her family at a casual restaurant when a bunch of young guys, who had apparently been drinking to excess, spotted her and begin pointing and calling out her stage name, trying to get her attention, basically, causing an embarrassing scene. You never know when you might run into people that you know nothing about, but who know that you are a stripper. Out with my kids, I find myself avoiding eye contact with strangers for fear of that chance recognition.

I'm not sure exactly what I'm worried about, someone yelling out, "Hey, aren't you a stripper?" in front of my kids? As unlikely as it is, I haven't told my children anything yet, and that is certainly not how I want the topic to be broached. My son is a light sleeper and hears me when I come in at 3:00 AM. When he asks, I tell him that I was working late at the office. Our team keeps crazy schedules, so it isn't out of the question, but I can tell he's suspicious that something else is going on. Luckily, *Mom is a stripper* is a pretty far-fetched alternative explanation.

What makes me feel "empowered" and free-spirited within the confines of the club, leaves me exposed and vulnerable in the daylight. I can tell that being recognized in front of her daughter bothers her more than she lets on. If she quits anytime soon, I'm sure this will be the reason.

We all start sounding off about the things that suck about this job and I mention how bad the money smells. They barely notice it now, but everyone has a comment about it.

"One time I was getting my nails done, and I overheard one of the manicurists talking about having to take sweaty money from the strippers that come in. I guess she didn't know that I pay with stinky stripper money too, Screw you bitch, at least I don't have to dig the gunk out of people's toenails for a living." We banter back and forth about the source of that smell - their breath, the smoke, and the sweat. The smell gets on everything just from being in this building.

"When I take my bag home and unzip it, the smell pours out of it and every piece of clothing needs to be washed whether it was worn or not."

"It's from their dirty hands. I take my purse on stage with me and don't let any of it actually touch me. When I worked in another club a few years back, some dancers would take dollars in their teeth or between their breasts, could you throw up?"

Our stories are halted, as one by one each of has to get out there to dance. I'm following Miranda tonight. I wouldn't dare ask Miranda how old she is, but I can tell she's been doing this a long time. Not that she looks old, just experienced. Miranda has very long red hair and freckles. She is extremely thin and exotic looking. It seems as though Miranda is always here at the club. I like to think of her as the James Brown of the strip circuit, the hardest-working woman in show business. From what I've seen so far, she appears to work every shift, and when she's done dancing, she waits on tables. The one time I don't see her on stage, in back, or on the floor waitressing, I hear that she is busy babysitting the manager's son.

I also notice that she only has a few outfits, which stands in stark contrast to the girls who couldn't possibly earn as much money as

Miranda, but seem to spend so much on more clothes. One is this blue and white polka dot sailor jumpsuit kind of thing, which certainly stands out, but is not nearly as hideous as it sounds. Miranda is more of a gymnast than a dancer, among her repertoire she does a backbend and walks around the stage on her hands like a crab. Personally, I don't see this as even remotely sexy, but it is quite fascinating, and she maintains a stable of hopelessly devoted regulars. When she isn't working them, she is sweeping the room soliciting table dances.

I'm convinced that Miranda could do anything she wanted to do in life. Along with a couple other dancers like her, she comes in, stays focused on the work, and wastes very little time talking to anyone who isn't paying her to do so.

Before coming to work here, I had always heard inflated estimates of what strippers earn and I assumed that their claims of anywhere from $500-1,500 a night were an attempt to justify doing something for a living of which they were not particularly proud. I'm sure in some clubs in New York or Los Angeles, these figures are entirely possible, but I made nowhere near that much. Granted, I am hardly aggressive, but for a variety of reasons - bad weather, sports events on TV, too many dancers on the floor, or just a slow night - big earnings are potential, but certainly not typical.

Miranda makes the most of the potential, and given her work ethic, a six-figure income is not out of the question. Also, there is nothing obvious about how she might be spending her money, she drives an older car (one of the few of us who has a car), and although she must have plenty saved up, none of us go around talking about how we spend our money.

I go out there in my brand new stripper shoes for the first time. I walk around the club looking for someone who might want to buy a table dance or ask me to sit for a drink. It's still too early for that and when I don't see anyone I head for the DJ booth to chat with whoever is on tonight and make my music selections clear. On the way over, I trip on this big lump in the carpet, and although I don't fall all the way to the floor, I flail and stumble around in a most undignified way. I receive the obligatory round of applause from onlookers close by, and then to their amusement, I curtsey to signify that I'm okay. In truth, I'm extremely embarrassed and worried that someone might

51

think I'm drunk. Lucky for me that lump in the carpet is notorious and no one said another word about it.

Later on stage, I miscalculate yet again exactly where that one-quarter-inch of a spike passing for a heel should be planted for me to remain upright and I nearly fall once more. Finding the right shoes is critical to this job. I can see now why they are so expensive and such a frequent topic of discussion around here. So much for getting used to them.

In these shoes? Honey, I don't think so.

The Daughters of Phorcys and Ceto

Graeae: The three "old women" or "gray ones" from Greek mythology. They are the daughters of Phorcys and Ceto, sisters and guardians of the Gorgons. They were gray-haired from birth and have only one eye and one tooth, which they share among them. They are Enyo ("horror"), Deino ("dread") and Pemphredo ("alarm").
— *Encyclopedia Mythica,*
    http://www.pantheon.org/articles/g/graeae.html

Initially, I was very excited about my career. The job itself is not too bad, but the hours are crazy, and I have yet to find my niche in this small, established group of mostly women. Things are still going very poorly, and my newest strategy has been one of avoidance. My office has a large window that faces the sun, and it can get unbearably hot in the afternoon. Even still, I keep my door closed until I am almost ready to pass out from the heat just to discourage anyone around who might want to stop in and talk to me.

It's after 6:00 and the Daughters of Phorcys and Ceto, as I have come to refer to them (though only to myself), have all left the office for the evening. They still barely speak to me. For my part, I've changed my desperate-to-be-accepted tactics so many times they probably think they're working with Sybil. The Daughters of P and C treat every one of my nineteen personalities with sheer contempt and undiluted condescension. I've never in my life been hated like this before, not even in junior high, and I spend more time obsessing over this than I have billable hours. Today, I successfully avoided a number of potential power struggles that I can't possibly win, so by successfully deflecting, I can count this day among my few victories by forfeit.

I can't tell whether the anti-depressants are making things better or worse. I feel petty and childish trying to explain why I feel so sad about my job. Lots of people have crappy jobs and you don't hear them whining about it. I think the biggest problem for me is the incongruity between what is said and what I feel.

"Refrigerator Mother" is the term used to describe the childhood experiences of schizophrenics, back when psychiatry erroneously blamed the victim's mothers for the disorder. It was presumed that these mothers would be smiling, with open arms, saying, "I love you," but their body language and affect would feel to the child just the opposite, cold and unloving. That is Lynne, a refrigerator mother.

When I got the feeling that I was not welcome, I came right out and asked. And, after a long talk, getting to know each other, exchanging friendly, but not too personal anecdotes, I was left to wonder how I could be so foolish and insensitive as to think Lynne was anything but a wonderful, benevolent force of purity and goodness. I must have completely misunderstood and misjudged the situation. Then, as she was closing the door behind her, she popped her head back in.

"You know, Cheryl, I don't have to *like* someone to work with them."

There were big red flags waving from the very beginning. I should have known better, but I mistook all the red flags to be just my usual insecurity, me being foolish and scared. I didn't trust my own intuition and thought I could make it work.

The ad for this job included an email address, and I immediately sent my resume and some writing and programming samples. After one phone interview that I did not perceive as having gone very well, I was summoned to Seattle to interview with the entire management litigation team.

The whole experience was strange and new to me, but since I had never been flown out for an interview or ever interviewed for a non-academic job, that is, other than food service or housekeeping, I can't say whether my experience was particularly unique. The man who was to be my immediate supervisor had to fly in from the East coast. To save money, the company planned a four-day stay over a weekend and made all the arrangements for my hotel and rental car. All expenses were paid, and I felt very grown up, uncomfortably so.

I began to feel much more like myself when the airline lost my luggage and the rental car agency didn't seem to have any record of the company's payment information. I had never driven in Seattle, and it was raining and dark, but eventually I made it from the airport to the hotel, sans luggage.

We had only emailed and spoken on the phone, but I had spent some time preparing for my interview by looking up everything I could find about my potential new boss, Dan, and the other consultants on the team. I found his dissertation and a number of academic publications, almost all of them concerning discrimination against African-Americans.

In one of his emails, Dan referred to himself as an "aging psychologist". Based on these two pieces of information, I expected to meet a distinguished African-American gentleman, graying at the temples. I opened the door to find a distractingly attractive dark-haired man, overly tan from his vacation immediately prior to this trip, but neither black, nor particularly "aged".

When I find myself in tense situations, justifiable or exaggerated by my demoralizing inner monologues, I occasionally have a problem that I like to call "free floating Tourette's Syndrome".

"Hey, you're not black!" Oh, God, I can't believe I just said that.

"Huh?"

"You're not that old either, how old are you?" Why do I keep talking?

I continue. "You said that you were an aging psychologist; I wouldn't call you aging...uh...at all." I keep going, explaining that I looked him up in academic library databases and based on how he had described himself and the topics of his journal articles, I was expecting to meet an old black guy. So now I'm racist and a stalker.

Please God, let him start talking. He does. He just got back from a trip to Key West with his daughter. He loves Key West, and he loves his daughter. He whips a picture of her out of his wallet to show me. His obvious doting on his only child is very endearing, and I finally relax a little as we walk in the cool night air to find a restaurant.

My luggage was delivered the next morning, and the rest of the weekend was spent with the two of us trying out restaurants around town. We weren't quite sure how to reimburse me for meals, plus I had nothing else to do, so there we were, breakfast, lunch and dinner, talking statistics, and getting into some very heated, and also loud, discussions about feminism.

Monday came, and it was time to meet the rest of the consultants. I couldn't sleep the night before, going over and over in my head what I might be asked and what I should and shouldn't say. By the time Dan and I headed for the office, I was already miserably exhausted.

When we arrived, no one from the team was in yet and wouldn't be for quite some time. Trying to be helpful, I offered to make coffee in what turned out to be a notoriously quirky industrial coffeemaker. Hot, black liquid sprayed all over, streaming down over the countertops and spilling onto the floor before I was able to make it stop. Some office folks came to help, explained that it wasn't actually my fault and amidst their amusement at the kickoff of my interview process, apologized for not stopping me from using the machine. Thankfully, Dan did not see any of this go on.

What followed was not unlike being marooned at a car dealership.

Although they had chosen the day to meet, all of the consultants were extremely preoccupied and could not seem to get themselves together with me all at the same time. After waiting through several hours, three room changes, and numerous interruptions, the interview process officially began. Having already heard more than enough from me, Dan had bailed out sometime along the way. The three women who make up the rest of the team asked me questions about my background and my dissertation and listened dispassionately to my responses while we waited for Dick, the CEO, to return.

I was so tired from lack of sleep and the agitation of endless waiting around — adrenalin rising each time I thought we were about to formally interview and then plummeting each time we were sidetracked. I started to wonder if there were men with lab coats and clipboards behind a two-way mirror somewhere nearby hastily taking notes on my response to this miserable experiment. I have no idea what I said, but I doubted that it mattered. By that time, I didn't care. I could tell almost immediately that I was collectively and forcefully disliked.

Lynne is very tall. Standing nearby, the other women look dwarfed. She is feminine, with wavy, auburn hair. Her features are delicate, emphasized with casual, understated make up that almost covers the faint remains of childhood freckles. Lynne is also quite heavy. When she sat down, I could see tangled webs of varicose veins straining up her legs beneath the hem of her skirt. Her feet were swollen and it looked painful.

Effusive and witty, she exudes southern boarding school manners and seems extraordinarily intelligent and confident. If I didn't perceive such an overwhelming sense of disapproval toward me, one to which I cannot attach anything objective and yet I would swear to, I think I could like her.

I am introduced to Mary Beth and Jane. They are either shy or standoffish toward me, probably both. Mary Beth is a frail, opaque woman with long, brown hair she wears in a tight bun at the nape of her neck. Her clothes are drab and baggy, meant for a woman much older than herself. Jane, a middle-aged woman who vaguely resembles Mr. Spock, offers a polite smile as she reaches out to shake my hand and motions toward the chair reserved for me.

They are both stiff. Like Lynne, their speech patterns and demeanors convey their shared educated, upper middle class, Anglo upbringing. In their defense, or rather to put this into context, there is not a single person of color in the entire building. Jane and Mary Beth are polite, but seem globally annoyed by the interruption of their day with my presence. Fundamentally, I can't remember the last time I felt more Jewish.

The intern came by, and we were introduced. Lisa recently completed her bachelor's degree at Portland State. She seems darling, but perhaps a little ditzy too, because as soon as she walks out the door, Mary Beth rolls her eyes and calls her a "black hole".

With this, I wanted to quickly, quietly end this endless interview and go home. I could've gone back to the hotel to get some sleep, but Dan had given me a ride in, and I didn't know how I would explain it to him without sounding like a nutcase or a giant crybaby, so I just kept on. By this time I felt sure it had to be almost over, but I was wrong.

I suppose they hadn't expected to begin hating me so quickly, because they planned for all of us, the consultants anyway, to have lunch together. The administrative assistant and Lisa had not been invited. With my hopes of a respite dashed, I looked around for Dan, who thankfully, wandered back around just in time to join us, but then barely spoke two words the entire time.

The waitress was one of those famed art district hippies, who moved as though she were walking through water, never making any eye contact, prolonging this pointless meal to the outermost boundaries of my emotional endurance.

Dan concentrated on his meal. Meanwhile, I listened to them discuss how much they hated a movie that I was shocked they had even seen. Faced with the chance to offer an alternative opinion, I bit my tongue. The less talk, the more eating, and the sooner the whole thing would be over, and I'd be on a plane home.

When we returned to the office, Dick was still not back, but they were through babysitting me. I had already heard a lot about Dick. He was supposed to be brilliant, arrogant, charming, egotistical, and very charismatic. I was excited and nervous to meet him.

They left me alone in Dick's office, and I waited there for three more hours. I spent some time talking to a computer tech who came in to load software or fix something. When he left, I scanned the bookshelves for something to read. Among the sets of academic journals, management textbooks, and books Dick had written himself was a cheesy detective novel - real shit. I got comfortable on his couch and began to read until I must have lay down and fallen asleep.

He put his hand out for me to shake it and to pull me upright.

"Hello, you must be Cheryl, I'm Dick. So, what do you think?"

"I think... I think it's fine?" My sleepy, brilliant response.

"So, what do you think of Dan? How has it been going so far?"

"Dan and I have been to every restaurant in the Seattle area. Yesterday, we went sightseeing. I drank so much coffee that Dan had to pull over three times to find me a bathroom. It's been like the longest date I've ever had without actually getting any sex."

I know. I can't believe I said it either, but I did. Either Dick wasn't listening, or he ignored me outright. He may have asked me if I wanted the job. I must have given an answer somewhere within the realm of the affirmative, because he wrapped it up by telling me that Dan should go ahead and call my references.

If I had been paying more attention to what was going on around me instead of focusing so intently on my own anxiety and discomfort, I might have actually learned something. Consequently, I might have made any number of better decisions than I did.

By the time I made it back to my hotel room, I had twisted the whole day around in my head until I convinced myself that I was doomed. I had given a horrible interview, I deserved to be treated rudely, I embarrassed myself, and I would never again get another decent job offer.

I took a bath and sat crying in it until the phone rang. It was Lynne wanting to close the deal. Thoroughly exhausted and distraught, this was the perfect time to talk money and of course, I couldn't help but settle for nothing less than rock bottom.

About five days later, Dan called to officially offer me the job. It turned out that I was the only person they interviewed. I didn't want to take it, but I did anyway. All I knew for sure was that I never wanted to go through another job interview as long as I lived.

Topless Therapy

Step right up and don't be shy
Because you will not believe your eyes
She's right here behind the glass
You're gonna like her cuz she's got class
You can look inside another world,
You get to talk to a pretty girl
She's everything you dream about
But don't fall in love
She's a beauty, She's a one in a million girl
She's a beauty, Why would I lie?
Why would I lie?
You can say anything you like
But you can't touch the merchandise
She'll give you Every penny's worth
But it will cost you a dollar first.
You can step outside your little world
You can talk to a pretty girl
She's everything you dream about
Why would I lie, Now why would I lie?
But don't fall in love
Cuz if you do you'll find out she don't love you
She's a one in a million girl
Why would I lie, now, why would I lie?
             — She's a Beauty Artist: The Tubes
             CD: The Completion Backward Principle

Tips In: $163
Tips Out: $35

I thought that when my family finally moved to Seattle to be with me, I'd at least have a happy place to come home to at night. As it turns out, we are all having some trouble making the transition.

At home, there is chaos. Unpacked boxes litter the otherwise empty apartment, and we dig through them furiously as items are needed. I'm amazed by people who can move themselves from one place to another, unpack, and have their new homes arranged and put together the very same day.

My husband, who has yet to find a job, is a little more into my dancing than maybe he should be. When I leave for my day job, he has my bag packed with big shoes, sexy outfits, and T-bars that he has hand-washed ever so lovingly and hung to dry. Tripping over cardboard boxes as I head out the door, I'm wishing he'd spend more time unpacking our stuff instead of laundering underpants and window-shopping for stripper clothes.

Everything is still so up in the air. Every day Allan has to drive Dmitri back and forth to his performing arts high school in Tacoma, and at least once a week, stop by the house where our dogs are boarded to clean up dog poops in the backyard. Although we are still looking for a house that won't be too expensive or too far from work, we had to settle Maria into a middle school near our temporary apartment. She's already anxious about making new friends and then possibly having to change schools once we find a home. We are all under a lot of stress, passing each other in the hall, but none of us really connecting.

With so much going on, the apartment, my house, currently unsold back home, Dmitri's tuition, new school clothes and heavy coats, and all of the hidden costs of moving and a new job, I feel like I am hemorrhaging money. When I decided to strip, I had no idea how much the extra money would come in handy.

I consider myself lucky that Allan isn't upset about my decision to strip. He trusts me, and I know he is tickled by the idea of his wife feeling sexy enough to do something like this. He's so supportive, but worries about the long drive home late at night or someone in the club becoming violent. We both worry about me getting recognized and subsequently fired.

On the flipside, I'm starting to get into the groove of the club and except for being tired and suffering from sore muscles, I look forward to it. In stark contrast to my real job, I feel welcome, and I frequently experience the camaraderie and teamwork that provides real-time profit to those who work together and to the larger organization.

Doormen tell us who has a wad of cash in his wallet, DJs tip us off to creeps or play a longer tune when the stage is full, bouncers keep their eyes open, we push for another round and order premium, waitresses water down our drinks and put the leftover in his, we make more, we share more, and everybody makes more money.

In this case, instant gratification is a good thing, immediate feedback and positive reinforcement for cooperation. They should start a side business sending stripper consultants out to human resource firms. Forget CORE, forget TQM, forget about searching for misplaced cheese. Honey, who moved my G-string?

I actually enjoy myself more on Mondays and Tuesdays than on busier, supposed big money nights. It feels less mercenary and more personal. You can sit and talk to people. Last night I had a man pay me for a private dance, but when he got me there he said all he wanted was to ask my advice about whether he should get back with a girl he had dated a while back but had moved away.

He's been lonely and she called him up and said she wanted him back. What should he do? I'm big on sorting out all the pros and cons and then just doing whatever it is you want to do while trying to minimize the identified cons. I think people do what they want to do anyway, so why put yourself through it? What did he have to lose? Would he have to move out there? Why not just plan a trip out, just to have some fun and see what happens?

A second song started, and he'd pulled out another twenty so he could keep talking to me. I took the money, but I insisted on taking my top off while we continued our discussion. For me, that's ethics. I'm not a licensed therapist but I am a professional stripper, so I figured that was fair. I did it sort of to be funny, but also because I guess I felt like the situation was pathetic and I didn't want him to *feel* pathetic. A man paying a completely dressed stripper to sit and listen to him at twenty dollars a song, that's about five minutes, is just plain sad. I wanted him to walk away feeling like a man.

I know some women here look at these men as dogs and they couldn't care less whether a bus hits one of them on the way home. Some define their night less by how much they made in absolute figures, but by whether they emptied some guy's wallet completely. They take pleasure in racking up the numbers of men whose resources they have completely depleted. Did you send him to the cash machine? Getting them to take more money out of the ATM up front just to hand over to you, I'm told, is a very gratifying experience. Some of the dancers date big spenders and continue the draining outside of work hours. Does this constitute a hobby? I like the money, but even if I weren't married, I couldn't go for that. I sense a distinct division between girls who attach no meaning whatsoever to the money in that they solicit and accept money for anything, everything, and also for nothing, and those girls who see it as a bounded set of exchanges within the confines of the club.

I got a taste of it the other night. Instead of hanging around in my office, I came in early. As Kara, one of the few African American women in the club was leaving, she pointed out the foreigner over at the bar who loves to spend money.

"I'm going off shift, but you should go get your share. Be careful because he will try to tongue-kiss you and feel you up."

The big spender's name is Aron and he hails from the former Soviet Union. He introduces himself to me as "the patron saint of strippers". I'm not the only girl there hanging on his every word and my competitive streak is showing.

He buys me a drink with a twenty-dollar bill and gives me the change. I decide to get pushy and ask him straight out for another five, and he smiles and hands it to me. Pretty soon, I've got $40 and a drink and I haven't even taken anything off. I like him already. When I go on stage, he sits smiling and drinking, constructing pyramids of dollar bills along the stage for me to take. Aron is dating one of the strippers and at first I assume that I should back off, but I'm new — I don't get it. Ronnie, his club girlfriend, meets up with him, and although she stands the closest to him, she doesn't shoo us away. As I come to understand, this is the deal. He takes one stripper as a girlfriend and buys her clothes and jewelry. They go to the club, and he acts like a big shot while they try to find another girl to join them overnight.

Ronnie claims to be younger than me, but I seriously doubt it. She uses a fluffy rug on stage to spare her knees. I'm dying to steal that idea, my knees are covered with painful bruises all the time, but I won't even though I doubt she'd mind. We over-thirty strippers need to stick together. Ronnie does a great job of acting like she really likes this guy. Aron is about fifty, tall and not at all bad looking. Twice the bartender pulled me aside to warn me about his hands.

"He spends a lot of money on you girls, so we let him get away with too much. Don't let him push it, or I'll kick you both out."

His accent is kind of cute. After he has given me quite a bit of money, I flash him my tits while we are in the smoking room. You're only supposed to show tits while on stage, so the bartender lectures me once more for doing it, but the compliment Aron gave me, I'll never forget: "Jewish girls have the nicest nipples."

Having grown up with all sorts of ridiculous stereotypes about Jewish women — how they are not attractive and don't like sex — finally here is a generalization that I can appreciate. Eventually, I leave him alone so other girls could profit more. When it comes to sheer avarice, at first I thought it was newer dancers vs. seasoned ones, but that isn't the case. There are new dancers who suck up money like vacuum cleaners without any thought to building a base of regulars and those who start slowly, watching what others do. By the same token, there are seasoned dancers who see men as the barrier between themselves and dollar bills, and some who are much attuned to minimizing drama, and maintaining a stable, long-term work life.

As for me, I can see myself behaving in any point on the continuum depending on the day. It is none of my business how anyone else wants to spend money. If they want to give it to me instead of their wives, kids, or their favorite charity that is their prerogative, but I take no pleasure in dwelling on it. I'm not quite there yet, but after a certain number of bad experiences with patrons, I suspect I might begin to lose my empathy towards customers as people and focus not on the contents of their characters, but solely on the contents of their wallets.

I'll Give You Five If You Get It Hard

We should consider every day lost in which we do not dance at least once.

— *Nietzsche*

Tips In: $362
Tips out: $51

There is a giggling, gal-bonding thing happening in the dressing room tonight. We goof around sharing stories and locker room humor. No one is crying, nothing has been stolen recently, Lydia has been fed, and Pandora has a full pack of cigarettes and a Red Bull & rum waiting for her just outside the dressing room door. Roxy, a lovely Latina woman with a harsh New York accent, waves her hands around and flies into a hilarious tirade about how every man these days can't wait to tell her that she looks just like Jennifer Lopez.

Jim and one of the bartenders carry in a big box of decorations for a Hawaiian Luau party tonight, and together we tape them up on walls and along the stages. As the place begins to populate, I go from table to table advertising the party that will start much later tonight. After flitting around for quite some time, and I finally plant myself at a table of some nice looking techie types.

They react to me with a peculiar lack of enthusiasm, as if they are not sure they should be seen talking to me. Hell-lo! Strip bar: Strippers! Evidently, they've run into their boss who has now joined them at their table under coerced invitation. I call a waitress over and coquettishly demand that they order another pitcher of beer. Before too long his status as their superior becomes irrelevant, and I gain a loud and loyal fan club.

One devotee begins to talk to me at length. Right away I blow the single, no kids lie. He works with digital video, and I ask him many questions on behalf of my son who is very interested in photography and animation. We start talking about more personal topics. Again, here is one more attractive, personable man with a very good job, hanging around in a strip club. He is no regular, but still, I'm baffled at the attraction to a place like this and all of the attention and money he is willing to spend on a married stripper.

After exhausting the subjects of websites dedicated solely to the mullet haircut, digital animation software, and never having enough random access memory, he begins to tell me the intimate details of his recent, bitter divorce. My guess is one of two extremes: either he has never discussed the divorce before or he has discussed it so many times that his friends will no longer listen to him.

"I never cheated on her, I never even thought about it. Things started to go badly, and we didn't do anything about it for at least a couple of years. We just kept going along. I thought it would get better, but it only got worse until we barely acknowledged the other was even in the room. She kept a journal and one day I read it. She wrote that she couldn't stand it when I touched her. Couldn't stand it when I touched her! Why would she just keep going along so long after writing something like that?"

I am stunned at the depth and delicate nature of the conversation and stumble to think of a response. I muster up something brilliant to say like, "I'm so sorry… No, I don't understand it either."

I change the subject to something sexual as quickly as possible, and we rebound into lighter subjects. I suggest a game of pool. I am a lousy pool player, so to make things fair, I have changed the objectives of the game ever so slightly.

"Your goal is to get the balls into awkward positions so that when it is my turn to shoot I have to stretch and lean over the table. You can either face me to look down my blouse or stand behind me to admire my ass." I pivot, smile, and point to the referenced body part as I explain the new rules. "I get as many shots as I want. If I do manage to knock a ball in, I jump up and down in celebration, and you get to watch me." This is my standard pool game shtick.

Surprise, surprise, I won, and he showed no more signs of melancholy. Now that I had a solid warmed up audience, complete with a built-in fan base, I was on a roll that couldn't be stopped.

My next set was in the smoking lounge, which almost invariably sucks. It's just a small stage with a mirror against the wall, no poles. People are usually too busy playing pool or talking to strippers who are bumming cigarettes from them. Not this time. Three drunken amigos sit down at my stage and when one gives me a dollar, I challenge the next to give me a five. When he gives me the five, I turn to the third, "Are you going to let him show you up? Honey, I can't bear to see that happen." Ten more dollars on my hip, and I circle back to the one dollar man in mock disgust. As I continue my musical theatre, their pickled peer pressure escalates resulting in the continued round-robin transfer of funds into my T-bar.

"Real men empty their wallets, baby, there is no shame in that... Awwww, YOU are my knight in shining armor, sweetie... Thanks so much. There's an ATM by the front door, no problem." I dance off the stage and all the way back to the dressing room to deposit my windfall.

I pay a visit to Jake, a DJ who is constantly trying to fool around with me, and every other girl in the club, I'm sure. I humor him, but I heard that one of the dancers is his girlfriend, and when he comes up from behind and rubs against me, I remind him once again not to set me up to get my ass kicked, thank you very much. Jake is a cute guy, but a smart ass who never plays exactly what I ask for. Music is extremely important to the atmosphere and features prominently in the quality of work life of the exotic dancer.

Speaking of that, we have a dancer, Emotion, who brings her own briefcase of carefully cataloged CDs. She plans out every song she wants played in a certain order for each set. One time Jake played something else, acting as if it was a mistake, and she refused to move an inch until he put her song on. When her set was over you could hear her yelling at him in the booth over the music.

After the smoking lounge, we rotate back to Stage One where the dancer gets her choice of music.

"I want *Brass in Pocket*. Jake, I want *Brass in Pocket*; you know I always tip you so play the song, okay?" He's pretending to be concentrating on something else and then turns to me and says, "You girls get money just for showing your tits, it is so unfair. Hey, I'll show you my penis for a dollar."

"I'll give you a dollar if you show me your penis *and* play my song." He whips out his dick, and I admire it for a few seconds then hand him a dollar.

I start to walk back down out of the booth, but I turn around and yell back at him, "I'll give you five if you get it hard!" He wants to take the deal, and tries to get my attention again, but it's too late, I'm already halfway back to my table of techies.

"Just play the song!"

I've danced and sweated off my last drink, and my new divorced friend buys me another one. I take one sip before it's my turn on Stage One again. We have an unwritten policy never to leave a drink at a customer's table or otherwise out of our sight. I have no concern whatsoever that these men might tamper with my beverage, but still I take it with me out of habit.

I am following Lana tonight and she makes a production of exchanging places with me on stage. She takes my hand and draws me onto the stage, but doesn't immediately let go, running the back of my hand softly across her cheek. Men respond especially generously to displays of same sex affection around here, so I play along and flirtatiously smile and push her long black hair away from her face. She puts her shoes on and before she leaves the stage, I stare into the eyes of a patron sitting near the exit steps while I reach down to squeeze her shoulder. Any girl-on-girl activity has some overwhelming magical power over these men, and he can't hand over his money fast enough.

Jake plays what is now my signature song, *Wait,* first up. It's busy and I have a full stage of customers. I take wide, heavy strides all around the stage to attract attention from every corner of the room. I pop open a buckle and pull a string in time with the music. My techies are cheering for me and I coax them to risk losing their table and come up to my stage to tip me. By the time Chrissie Hynde belts out "*I got brass,* my black vinyl top flies off as I spin around, *in pocket.*" I am Trinity, queen of the pocket protectors!

I make my way around the stage, kneeling close to the edges of the stage and cradling my breasts with my forearms to push them up and out farther. Using one of the poles to steady myself, I bend over as far as I can and catch the eyes of a customer behind me on the opposite corner. I stomp my feet and make such a spectacle of myself that it seems that every pair of eyes is on me. I can hear chanting from my new fan club, "You go, Trinity! Trin It TEE! Trin It TEE! Trin It TEE!"

Within my larger than life dance routine, I still manage to give every one sitting at the stage some personal attention, bending over, lingering eye contact, or leaning in and whispering, "Thank you" as I pick up my tips. I grab my clothes, a few high fives, and a couple extra bucks floating around, and I get ready to pull the next dancer on stage. Jake calls into the microphone, "Trinity to the DJ booth." At first I think I'm in trouble for being so wild on stage, but then I hear him add, "And bring that five bucks."

Sometimes a Cigar is Just a Cigar

If you cannot get rid of the family skeleton, you may as well make it dance.

— George Bernard Shaw

Tip In: $141
Tip Out: $25

We're again forced to huddle together in a conference room, plugging away on a project that I think is ill-conceived and misguided, but I'm doing as I'm told and these days opening my mouth only to exchange civilities and work-related dialogue. I've been feeling sorry for myself, because I don't feel as though I am ever going to have any meaningful input into these cases and specifically in the project we are working on right now. I feel as though my expertise is being overlooked, or worse yet, seen, but completely disregarded.

Lynne and Dan don't get along and, lucky me, I answer to both of them. I've tried to find ways to mediate between them, but by the sheer nature of their power struggle, the depth of their particular animosity toward each other, it's a lose-lose situation for the poor schmuck who has to deal with it. I'm frustrated and bored. I still get paid regardless, so I suppose it shouldn't matter too much to me. As long as I keep focused and don't take it personally when I am caught in the firing line, it'll work out eventually.

It is after six, but there is no point in going all the way home before I go to dance. I'd have to turn right back around to get there with enough time to get ready, so I stay in the conference room until the last of them finally leaves, and then I hang out in my office and write emails and amuse myself by rooting around on the internet for nothing in particular until its time to go.

On the days I don't forget what I'm doing here, I ask my "question of the night". Tonight's is banal, nonetheless de rigueur. Why did you become a stripper?

Talia is the first to answer. Talia, who joined us just a few days ago, is both the newest and the oldest stripper at the club, claiming to be thirty-seven. She recently bought a brand new truck, but found that she can't make the payments. To me, an obsessive-compulsive credit report slave, this is what it means to truly live on the edge. Talia had jumped into the groove too quickly for this to be her first time, so I press her on it.

"I left home at sixteen and I had boyfriends here and there to help out. I went to go get a waitressing job, but ended up dancing because there was so much more money in it." She continued, "I liked having nice things and taking trips. I like being able to afford the things that I want and not have to depend on anyone else to get them for me. I couldn't afford nice clothes or my apartment working at the mall or flipping hamburgers."

Not entirely myth, a few dancers are, in fact, college students. The higher rate of return per hour is the biggest draw for all us whether we want to buy nice things, pay for college, or make enough money to support, but still have time for, our children.

I needed money and a girlfriend of mine was already doing it and got me started.

They took the job for the money, and anesthetized their initial misgivings with alcohol. Each of the dancers had only minor variations on this theme. Most had grown up poor or working class, alone with their mothers if they were lucky; if unlucky, their mother's boyfriends. If present, their relationships with biological fathers were not necessarily positive, but I did hear an exception that surprised me. One long time dancer maintains a good relationship with her father, who also happens to be a full professor at an Ivy League institution. However; I did not get the impression that this had always been the case.

Jess Belle, wagging her finger in the air, responds to the discussion of family histories, "Nothing will piss me off faster than some shithead talking pitiful to me and asking me if I do this because I'm looking for my daddy. Trust me; I would never look for my daddy." Someone interjects, "If anything, I did this to get the hell away from my daddy!"

74

I am surprised at the extreme consensus on this point, and I'm not sure I believe it. I look around for Katrina or Miranda, wondering if they might have a more positive spin to share, but they are nowhere to be found. I ask, "Are you trying to tell me that every single woman here had a terrible childhood?"

Emotion makes this pronouncement, "I'm telling you that every single stripper in this place has either been sexually abused, physically abused, or comes from a broken home. Now which one are you?"

Me? Wait a minute. I ask the questions around here. And besides, I'm not really a stripper anyway. As I am about to vehemently deny that any of these categories apply to me, I hesitate. She prods me, "You've thought of one, haven't you?"

Just when I think I am about to be done in by my own question of the day, it's my turn on stage. I set my sights on the big, gleaming poles at the four corners of the stage. It's not that I don't make use of them, I do. I swing and spin around and lean on them to regain balance or to slow things down. And when I can put the thought of how long it must have been since someone last cleaned and disinfected them completely out of my mind, I'll even go so far as to squeeze my breasts together around the pole in a move that is both trashy and undignified, but profitable. Still, when it comes to poles, I'm a piker. The pole, it mocks me.

Tonight I follow Jess Belle, who knows her way around these big, shiny, imitation brass poles as well as anyone else here. She is young, foul-mouthed, drug-abusing, trailer-trash. Jess Belle is tall and not quite plump, but curvy in the hips. The phrase that comes to mind is "corn-fed."

She once told me a story about how she spent ten days in a D.C. jail cell for illegal possession of Xanax. Some loose pills at the bottom of my purse make us fast friends. She is ignorant and cheap, but also very funny and nice. Jess Belle is the epitome of another observation that Emotion once mentioned to me, "The thing about strippers is that they may be bitches, or they may be slutty and dumb, but they are the first to admit it. They pretty much like themselves for who they are and what they don't like about themselves, they don't take out on you." Emotion should seriously consider writing a *Chicken Soup for the Stripper*.

When I get on the stage I complain to Jess Belle that I can't hop up and spin around on the poles. I want to, but I don't know how, and I'm afraid that I'll fall and crack my head open. Acknowledging this distinct possibility, she shows me what to do in steps.

"First, grab a spot on the pole up high and rub your hands on it up and down to create friction. It'll keep your hands from slipping around. Then plant your hands on that spot, and in one motion, jump as you pull yourself up with your arms, then wrap your legs around the pole and lock your knees. You hold on kind of like a monkey. Once your knees are locked, lean all the way back. Then you can let yourself slide back down until your shoulders meet the stage." She demonstrates it for me as the few customers nearby look on.

"Okay, I'm going to try it." I rub my palms on the pole until it isn't slippery anymore. I'm trying to concentrate, but I can't get over that the word "friction" somehow made it into her limited vocabulary. The 'grab on and pull myself up' part is a success, but I fail to adequately commit to locking my knees. That's okay; I can feel what wasn't quite right on the last try and try again. Strictly for the amusement of those watching who are privy to my mildly phobic concern about germs, I pantomime the spray cleaning and wipe down of the pole before I make my next attempt.

This time I feel my own strength and know approximately where the backs of my knees will need to land if I am to be safely perched on this pole. It's all one swift motion and my knees are locked, more like clenched, but either way I feel secure enough to release my hands and slowly lean back. I'm upside down, excitedly calling for Jess Belle, who has since shifted her attention to a paying customer, to look at me.

"Look, look, I did it! Look, you taught me how to do it!" I see some of my computer geek groupies and wave at them from upside down, and then let myself slide down. I do it a few more times during my set, but it's very tiring and the sliding down part stings the backs of my knees. Playing around on the poles looks great, and I'm proud of building my confidence and overcoming my fear. I can cross the poles off my to-do list, but I think it hurts more than it's really worth.

When my set is over, I go wash my hands and freshen up. I sit down with a group of men at a table not far from the stage. Three of them work in the same company, and one is a friend of theirs in from out of town. It seems that most of our customers are from out of town. I solicit a drink from the youngest of them and settle in to try and get one to invest in a table dance.

They want to know all about me. Yes, I'm married. I almost never lie about that and it does cost me tips. I've tried, but I'm such a terrible liar that when they ask and I say no, I'm told I get a weird look on my face and giggle involuntarily. Yes, I'm new. No, I don't date customers.

They're not interested in buying a table dance, but I don't feel like moving on to another table either, so I relax and we chat for a while. I tell them about having recently purchased my first new car, a sensible Honda Accord, and we all agree it is a solid purchase. A new dancer comes on stage, and they stop talking for a minute or so to watch her. One of them turns to the younger man closest to me and remarks that the dancer's legs are too big. He doesn't think she is very attractive. I'm annoyed by his comment, but I keep it light and reply that I think she is curvy and sexy, and does he need his glasses or what?

"She is fat, her ankles are thick, and her boobs are kind of small compared to the rest of her. You are much prettier than her." He was picking her apart as though she were nothing more than the sum total of her body parts. Tits + ass + legs + hair + face = stripper.

"Do you think that I'm flattered by that?" I'm upset and insulted. I want to say, "And you can say this because you are the finest specimen of manhood on the planet?" or "You couldn't be with a girl like her even in your wildest dreams." I want to call him a pencil dick and throw a drink in his face for having the nerve to judge her that way. I'm not defensive about her personally — I don't even know her. This pompous prick is judging whoever is on that stage, including me, and probably every other woman he comes into contact with regardless of her occupation. When all was said and done, I ended up not saying anything.

I pick up my drink and leave briskly as though I have just seen someone standing on the other side of the room with whom I urgently wish to speak. I find Pandora in the smoking room and regale her with the ever so slightly embellished tale of my recent conquest of the magnificent, menacing pole.

If a Tree Falls in the Forest...

If there are ions in the solution, and there are no counter-ions around to stabilize it, does it really have a charge?
— *Neal, http://web.mit.edu/knz/www/new/nerdquotes.html*

Tips In: $80
Tips Out: $15

I went to the library today to collect some articles for a case. Libraries are among my favorite places to be. I have no sense of direction whatsoever, but I can always find my way around the library. Reference materials retrieval is Lisa's job, but she is out of town this week, so I volunteered. Mary Beth was surprised that I would want to do that, expressing her belief that library scut work is beneath those of us with advanced degrees.

Except for photocopying, I much prefer doing my own library searches. I need to be able to scan book titles, and skim articles, letting them lead me to even better sources along the way. No one can do that for you just the way you would. I brought back all the requested materials, plus a few more good articles, then got ready to go to job number two.

There is probably some sporting event going on tonight because the club is virtually empty. I am one of three dancers on the floor, and there is one customer in the entire building, and rather than be nearby at my stage, he is standing over at the bar. Like the tree that falls in the forest when there is no one there to hear it, I am required to dance whether or not anyone is there to tip me.

The music is funky, and I start goofing around trying out a few urban dance moves that my kids taught me as a joke. I spin in wide circles doing 'the sprinkler' and 'opening the coffee can' and striking all varieties of gangsta-rap poses. I get nothing. Not even a courtesy laugh, so I mix it up a bit and switch to my special brand of 60's dance craze moves. Out of boredom, I've had my two and a half drinks early tonight. In a sing-songy voice, I call out to the one man at the bar to please, please come over to my stage.

He pretends he doesn't realize I'm talking to him for as long as he can, but I don't let him off the hook. I badger him until the situation threatens to become an embarrassing scene, embarrassing for him anyway. He gives in and comes over near the stage. I guess he thinks I'm desperate for his dollar so he hands me one. I accept it, but explain that the only thing more pathetic than dancing around and disrobing for strangers is dancing around like a moron and disrobing for nobody at all.

I use the opportunity to get off my feet and recline on the stage in a position where it looks like I'm still dancing, but I'm really just having a conversation. When my set is over, we find a table and talk for a long while. Despite a major faux pas early on in which he casually mentions that he can tell I have children by the stretch marks on my stomach, I am frantic for some attention so I continue talking to him. At some point much later I realize that I have committed the almost unforgivable sin of keeping a customer, mind you, the *only* customer, occupied away from the stage where he could potentially be tipping. I poke at him to send a couple bucks their way so we can keep talking.

As it turns out, he has a Ph.D. in physics. He shows me his business card and I run to the dressing room to get my own from my purse. I have not discussed my background or the details of my day job with anyone at the club until now, but I make an exception not only due to loneliness and boredom, but also because of my excitement to reminisce about finally finishing school with someone who has jumped through similar hoops. We discuss at length the rigors, absurdities, and idiosyncrasies of finishing our respective academic programs. Inevitably, he asks, but again I manage to evade answering the question of what I am doing here.

His prodding, though gentle, reminds me of my last question of the day and how Emotion volleyed that one right back at me without skipping a beat. Not only did I weasel out of answering her, but I also managed to convince myself that any further acknowledgment of my own discomfort with the question was a threat to my anthropological distance and professional objectivity. It takes years of education and self-discipline to be this incapable of grasping the obvious.

Bob has been coming to this club for way too long. He's embarrassed about how often he's come in and how much money he's spent over the years. He's lonely, and I think it makes him feel better that at least he has some good stories to show for it. He tells me one about this Russian immigrant who pretends to have much more money than he really does. This guy once got kicked out of here for hopping on stage and exposing himself.

"They let him stay, because he throws a lot of money around. I heard he once ran out of cash and handed out checks to the girls and the checks bounced." Good thing I don't take checks.

A few more customers make their way into the club. A man with a bandana tied over his head is sitting at the edge of the one stage that is open. It's almost time for my next set and a bouncer leans over to me, pointing at him. He warns me about the guy, but doesn't say why.

"I'll be watching. If he tries anything, if you feel uncomfortable, just look at me, and I'll take care of it." Well shit, by the time I get up there I'm a nervous wreck, but I try to dance as I normally would. There are only four customers around the stage now, and they are not cracking out many bills. Bandana man gets my attention, and I dance to the edge to take his money. As I'm holding out the side of my T-bar for him to place the dollar, he is still folding it. He folds the dollar three times making it small enough to place on his fingertips, dragging them against me as he tips. I wave my finger at him playfully, though I was disgusted and angry, and look at the bouncer who comes over and chastises him, but doesn't remove him from the bar. For the next song he waves dollars at me, but I don't come back. I don't need the dollar that badly. As I take Jess Belle's hand and trade the stage, I tell her to stay away from him.

"Stick around. I'll show you how we handle dicks like this guy when the fucking bouncers won't."

She teases him and circles the stage four or five times, taking money from everyone but him. He is practically begging her to come over and take his dollar bills — by now a whole three dollars! Again he folds one bill twice more than is acceptable, positioning the money in such a way that as he places it, he can run his fingertips against her hip. She lets him do it and then smiles directly at me as she swiftly kicks his beer over, spilling it into his lap, and snatching up the other two bills he dropped on the bar. He exits the club yelling at her, but without need of any additional bouncer assistance.

STRIPPER SHOES

Jess Belle is quite a character. One Saturday a few weeks back, I witnessed my very first drug transaction when she was on stage. A skinny, but rough looking young man walked right up to the empty stage where she was dancing and instead of him handing her a dollar bill, she handed him one that was crumpled up in her hand. He went to sit at a table nearby and I saw him open it up gingerly so that whatever the contents, they wouldn't fall to the floor. He returned to the stage and handed her some bills just as if he were tipping. That was the first and only incident of this type that I was aware of, but that doesn't mean it didn't go on. I couldn't wait to get home to tell my husband about my latest adventure.

Territorial Disputes

I find it rather easy to portray a businessman. Being bland, rather cruel and incompetent comes naturally to me.

— *John Cleese*

Tips In: $112
Tips Out: $15

Maybe it *is* harder to work with women. Wherever I go these days, tensions are high. A sort of class warfare has been building up around me in the office, the Daughters against Cathy, the secretary, and Lisa, the intern. For the most part, it has to do with exclusion from conversations and work luncheons, and being talked down to and talked about.

Unlike the Daughters of Phorcys and Ceto, Cathy and Lisa are friendly to me, which, of course, puts me on the losing side of this undeclared war. I try to clear the air and find some common ground, but it always backfires, making things worse, or kicking off a whole new ridiculous catfight, it never ends.

Though today, for a few blissful minutes, I thought I finally had this Daughters of Phorcys and Ceto thing figured out. It was a three-part solution that had to do with the weather, my hair, and neo-nazism.

Most of the time I straighten my hair with a blowdryer because I think it gives me a more professional, put together look, but today, it rained. When it rains, my hair shrinks in length, but doubles in width. Any attempts to manage it only makes matters worse. This morning when Lynne, flanked by her henchwomen, asked me if my hair was naturally curly, I said, "Sort of, it's a combination of genes and humidity." She paused, looked right through me and said, "If all those curls were natural, then we'd *really* hate you."

I was stunned mute as they blew past me, continuing on their way. Years ago, during my particularly awkward early teen years in rural Minnesota, a group of farm boys who were apparently fascinated by Hitler, menaced and hassled me relentlessly until high school, when I moved away. "Jew girl with nigger hair" was one among many, equally clever, but often much nastier, taunts that I had no choice but to ignore.

When Lynne teased me, the first thing I thought after, *Oh my God, I can't believe that bitch just said that to me*, was, *Oh my God, they hate me because I'm Jewish!* I felt so relieved, I mean, it had been such a long time since I'd even thought about this sort of thing, but with this, I've had plenty of practice. This I could handle.

If it were true and they did hate me because I'm a Jew, then that would mean I could stop trying to make them like me. I could stop trying to figure them out and stop trying to fix it. I was completely oblivious to the fact that I could stop all this regardless. I wanted to believe it so badly that for a few brief, fleeting moments, I actually had myself convinced, and it felt great.

If I could have maintained that belief, that anti-Semitism was at the core of my problems, it would have made my life so much easier. Unfortunately, I knew deep down it wasn't true. Maybe they are jealous of my new body and the confident way I have been carrying myself lately. Maybe Lynne meant to try and give me a compliment and it came out, well, it came out the way it did. Who knows, maybe it was gentile humor and I just didn't get it.

Zoot Allures Gentlemen's Club is not immune to petty jealousies, caste systems, and skirmishes either, but they tend to be more directed and short-term, based on seniority and, of course, money. Katrina is a dancer with seniority, whatever that may mean here. Even on slow nights at the club, she almost never talks to me. She isn't rude and I don't feel snubbed, but I am somewhat intimidated and I keep a polite distance. Katrina is tall, has very shiny, dark, just above shoulder length hair and dresses with impeccable taste. She is pretty, in a preppy, old money fashion. Think young Jackie O. A little on the stiff side, you would never guess that she is a stripper when not on stage, and barely so even when she is.

I've become so intrigued with Katrina that I ask Paul what he knows about her. He says since turnover is so high, Katrina never bothers to get to know people. She doesn't like to waste her time. She was working here when he started more than ten years ago, and he doesn't know any more than I do. She's a private person. She shows up, on time, does her job, and goes home.

He has almost no additional information on her to share, which is especially surprising because Paul is the definitive source of reliable gossip at the club. The only full-timer among part-timers with grander aspirations, Paul has been bartending and managing the club for years as dancers, bouncers and DJs have come and gone. With his dry, sarcastic wit that is too often wasted here, he is the solid, unaffected, unwavering center of the club.

In any environment, I gravitate toward people like Paul. He's self-deprecating and funny, if not caustic. He's seen the same embarrassing dramas unfold many times over and is wholly unimpressed, now barely bothering to be amused by them. I suspect he makes a fairly decent income, but if he has a social circle, which I sincerely doubt, he would avoid admitting how he earns it. I've also noticed that Paul never leers or comes on to us the way the DJs and the doormen sometimes do. This alone makes him far more interesting to me than any of the other men who work here.

One evening I find Paul sitting in the smoking room on his night off. I am surprised he would want to hang around here when he didn't have to. He looks so different in his street clothes, smaller and younger. I sit down next to him and ask him questions, but he is quick to deflect them and turn them around on me. From years of being a bartender, he must be more comfortable listening than talking.

He's not married, and he doesn't have a girlfriend. I don't ask him if he's gay, but I don't think so. For one thing, a gay man would find this place uncomfortable and annoying on too many levels to list. I smoke a cigarette with him and turn my back to everyone else in the room. Though he'd never admit it, Paul seems to enjoy my undivided attention. He's leaning on the bar, looking off at nothing in particular in the next room. With me in his peripheral vision, he exhales smoke as he talks to me, "You don't seem like the typical dancer starting out."

"I'll bet you say that to all the girls." I try to play him off, but part of me is dying to impress him.

"Yeah, no, really. What are you doing here?"

As much as I hate small talk, I'm in no mood for a truly honest conversation.

STRIPPER SHOES

"Making money with my giant tits. What are you doing here?" is my snappy retort, "It's your day off. I'd think this is the last place you'd want to be."

"My landlord fumigated the apartment house, I'm killing time while it airs out. When did you pick up smoking?"

"A few weeks ago. I only do it while I'm here. My husband would kill me if he finds out so I keep the pack in the DJ booth to share. It's hard to hang around here without smoking."

"Tell me about it."

We pass the time, smoking and staring at nothing in particular.

"Are you here every day?" I ask.

"Pretty much. You said you have a day job, what do you do?"

"I'm a statistician. It's kind of like being a programmer, but I also do data analysis."

"Sounds interesting." He nods approvingly. I can tell he believes me, probably because if I were making something up, I'm sure I'd make up something better than that.

"Sometimes. I moved here from Tucson to take this job, but so far I'm not very happy. People there are mean to me. I like working here much better."

"So, you're what…thirty? You've got a good job and you work here at night because they're mean to you?"

"No, I work here because I want to. I'm writing a book about a woman experiencing a mid-life crisis who decides to become a stripper."

"Ahh, that's right, you're not really a stripper. She's a singer, he's a filmmaker, I'm the only one here who actually works in a nudie bar."

"Well…here I am where no one knows me. There doesn't seem to be a better time to try this. I wanted to drop a few pounds, plus I couldn't think of anything interesting to write about. This is interesting, right?"

"I guess if you've never been in a strip club, it could be interesting, but I don't buy it. You could write about anything. I think you want to be a stripper and are just using writing about it as an excuse to take your clothes off."

I don't know how to respond. I feel attacked or at least insulted. Paul is implying that I want to strip and manufactured a justification

86

for it after the fact. I'm not sure he is entirely wrong, but even in my own confusion about my motives, I am not prepared to concede the point. I *am* prepared to admit that I am not sure what I am doing here. I'm lost, but if I keep good notes maybe I can follow them back like breadcrumbs. I begin to worry that what is bothering me about his comment is not that he is calling me a liar, but that he is calling me a stripper.

Between sets Katrina can always be found in the dressing room reading her books. I'm changing my clothes and she is sitting comfortably in the dressing room reading, when Miranda comes in looking for someone with whom to discuss her version of some prior unpleasant dealings with another dancer. Surprisingly, Katrina puts her book aside and encourages her to disclose. I'm not a part of the conversation, but there is no attempt made to exclude me, so I slow down the process of fixing my hair and make up and listen in.

Miranda claims she isn't really angry, but is clearly seething. She describes the events of the prior shift, repeating a number of points, as she talks herself into becoming more and more furious. Her issue boils down to one central transgression. Samantha, a girl who should know better, allegedly lingered around one of Miranda's regulars too long and managed to extract money from him that according to Miranda, rightfully belongs to her.

As she winds down, Samantha wanders in and begins a conversation with Miranda while Katrina and I pretend to be busy and oblivious. Miranda's tone of voice leads Samantha to ask her if she is upset with her about something and Miranda flatly denies any such thing. Dancers walk in and out of the dressing room, and we go about our business.

Eventually, Samantha must have been told or figured out what was wrong. From the bar I stand and watch Samantha try to talk to Miranda as she dances on an otherwise empty stage. Miranda ignores the display as long as she can, even after Samantha begins to throw bills on the stage at her.

"Is this enough? How about some more?" She throws more money down.

"How's this?" This goes on for a while, and I expect to see my first cat fight. Miranda is red-faced, and they both speak tentatively and too quiet for anyone to hear, but I can read the body language of negotiation. Miranda leans down and hugs her with one skinny freckled arm and, almost as quickly as it began, it is over. The pile of money remains on the stage until Miranda's set is over when she scoops it up and adds it to her stash.

Bald Is Beautiful

No one can make you feel inferior without your consent.

— Eleanor Roosevelt

Tips In: $120
Tips Out: $25

"My dreams are all about shaving." This unsolicited pronouncement is met with glares as the rest of the dancers fix up their hair and get dressed. What? Everyone else is not preoccupied with shaving? Maybe they are all naturally smooth and hairless, but for me, it feels like my whole world is beginning to revolve around shaving. And I'm not kidding; it's creeping into my dreams. Only slightly worse than reality, it grows as fast as I shave it, and I can't keep up.

I guess it's the equivalent of running away from a monster as your legs begin to feel like lead weights. In my waking life, I'm a hairy girl. Hairier than average I think. I have to shave everything before a shift. I squat and bend over in front of my husband and he shaves whatever stray hairs I miss. He thinks it looks fantastic, but I growl if he comments on it. On days I won't be dancing, it itches as it starts to grow back in. Take my word for it; do not try this at home. It is miserable, and I hate it.

This isn't a good time to start a conversation. I can sense any more comments from me will continue to hit the floor like bricks, so I shut up and get myself dressed. The dressing room is hot and crowded, and Pandora isn't here so there is no place to put my bag. Both my bag and I are constantly in the way. Getting herself ready, Delilah makes a plea to the rest of us, "Does anyone have any really light face powder?" Eager to be the one to help, I hand her my compact. She opens it up and examines it briefly before grimacing and handing it back to me.

"You shouldn't buy such cheap make up. This stuff is full of preservatives. If you bought a better brand like Lancôme you wouldn't have those wrinkles around your eyes."

Thank you very much, you nineteen-year old bitch.

I stuff my bag under the counter as far as I can and go pay for my own drink until it's time to get on stage.

I didn't start out in a bad mood. Usually I am thrilled to get in here. I like having a drink to loosen up, and I love the dancing, but tonight, especially after that thoughtful comment from the queen of sensitivity, I feel like an outsider. I'm closing in on twice the age of most of these girls, and I am feeling every minute of it. I am so tired, my legs are covered with bruises from the hard floor of the stage, and my knees hurt so badly that I can barely walk after working two shifts, two days in a row. Much more of this and I really will need a cane. I'm drinking more than I'm used to, and perhaps it is only the power of suggestion, but the lines around my eyes do seem especially prominent in the mirror tonight.

The good thing is that there really isn't time to ruminate or sulk. It'll be my turn to dance again soon and with this low lighting they can't see the lines or the bruises. Marcus puts on Beast of Burden just for me and I pull myself together and have some fun on stage. I'm taking bills and swinging around the poles and when I catch myself in one of the big wall mirrors, I can hardly believe that dancer is me. I may not be 19, but I'm trim and tight and I look great. I stand up straight and tall for a few seconds. I don't want anyone to notice me admiring myself in the mirror, but I stall by running my hands down my sides as I view my image from far away. I'm impressed and it takes my mind off feeling ugly and insecure. I move like a real stripper.

For a few seconds when I catch a glimpse of myself on stage, I feel really, truly great. I am as good as I want to be, and it doesn't matter whether I'm underfoot or if anybody likes me or how behind I am on laundry and shopping or whether I remembered to sign a permission slip or help with math homework or whether someone at work has it in for me or if its all in my head. There I am, just me, all by myself on stage. I'm tired and sore as hell, but if I can't be in bed asleep, this stage is not the worst place in the world to be tonight.

Cunning Linguistics

In my sex fantasy, nobody ever loves me for my mind.

— Nora Ephron

Tips In: $140
Tips Out $25

An unexpected perk of the industry is the very real chance that a sexy foreigner will offer American dollars to let him give me oral sex. The next best thing being an ugly American making the same hard-to-refuse offer. In the real world that hardly ever happens, and I think it's a shame. Like getting carded at a liquor store, it's always nice to be asked.

It's a pretty slow night, only a few paying customers and some regulars who belong to other dancers. I'm in a fantastic mood. I'm halfway through gin and tonic number two and warming up on my second set on stage. It's slow enough to linger as I move around the stage, and I lean down to make contact with a rugged looking man with long golden brown hair pulled back into a ponytail. He's been giving me a lot of attention and I'm soaking it up. When I ask if he'd like a private dance, I halfway expect him to brush me off. They're always so eager to get close to me until it's time to pay, then it's, "maybe later, you'll be the first to know," but this one is ready to go.

He takes me by the hand as we stroll to the stage area for a private dance. I feel warm from the gin and sway easily to the music. He lays $50 on the table, sits down and leans forward, never taking his eyes off me. I reach around him, gently touching the back of his neck and slowly pulling the elastic away, running my fingers through his hair.

He has that sexy, looser-than-British accent, but I can't tell whether he is from New Zealand or Australia. Either hates being called the other, so I ask. He's thrilled that I knew better than to guess that he is English. Kiwi it is. He has a rumpled, outdoors-all-the-time tan and great smile that show off his crinkly crows feet that are somehow flattering on foreign men like this guy and Sean Connery. He's already paid for an extra song and then some and I'm glad. I would have gone over either way, but I like him even more for not being cheap.

At twenty bucks a song, they sure are passive about what they'd like to see. Obviously I can't just sit there and stare at them, I have to move around, but it is hard coming up with stuff to do. I refuse to do a routine and stick to it like some kind of robot. Private dances are not unlike posing for art students, you have to come up with poses and change them periodically. At first I tried to be creative, but when you know you will be holding still for twenty minutes to an hour, you quickly learn to improvise on "reclining".

If I were paying that much for five minutes of someone's time, I'd probably bring a list. But I understand. They enjoy the idea of someone else thinking of things to do for once. They want to believe that I am spontaneously motivated to contort my figure in unlikely erotic positions, showcasing my various parts in hopes that I've made the most of their favorite.

Maybe that's where I go wrong. They have no favorite — they just like it. We spend so much time obsessing over single body parts, without realizing that real men like everything. Your thighs are fat? So are that dancer's over there, but she just got forty dollars to jiggle them in his face and he wants to see more. If you like it, they'll like it. If you show it off, they'll want to see it. It's all in the attitude.

I put my hands on his shoulders and squeeze, then run my palms down his chest and over his muscular thighs. I can't take my eyes off him as I sit on the platform between his legs and lean back, pulling off my lacy top. I rock myself on to my knees and lean forward, pushing my breasts close to his face. He grins at me, "You are so beautiful, I wish I could touch you." I wish he could touch me too, but he can't. I'm the right combination of buzzed and interested, but I don't want to lose my job. I turn away from him and get on my hands and knees. Arching my back a little, I try out a stripper trick I'd heard about through a friend of my husband's who would know these things. I grab the back of my thong and pull it tightly against my skin, exposing my skin around the thin strip of fabric. He can see almost everything. I let out a little whine.

"You are so beautiful," he says quietly, "I'd love to kiss your pussy. If we weren't here, would you let me go down on you?"

I smile and keep moving. I feel light-headed and warm, aroused and breathless. Feeling pleasantly liquefied, I lean against the mirror behind me and stretch my arms up, crossing them and letting them rest on the back of my head. He tells me what he'd do to me if I'd let him.

"I want to please your body. I'd lay you down, and make you feel so good, I promise. I'd touch you gently all over. I would stroke your thighs, parting them so slowly that you would barely even notice. I'd kiss you all over." I take another sip of my drink, "Uh hmm, that sounds wonderful."

"I'd love to lick you and watch you as you cum on my mouth." I swear it sounds a lot less dirty with an accent.

"Would you like me to do that? Would you let me?" I pause too long considering, which makes him think I am, well, considering.

"C'mon, you like me, I can tell. I am staying at the Sorrento. We can order some champagne, some dessert —"

"I'm sorry, it sounds absolutely wonderful, but I really can't go."

"We'll have a wonderful time."

"I'm not allowed to do that, I'm sorry." I don't know why I'm apologizing, but he keeps talking, "I can pay you, would you let me if paid you?" I can't help it, I laugh.

"I just want to go down on you, you wouldn't need to do anything for me, how about fifty dollars? A hundred?"

"I'm not a prostitute," I say quietly, still posing and writhing in front of him.

"No, I didn't mean that, I'm sorry, you are so gorgeous, I just thought it would be great to taste you. I'd love to do that to you." I know I should lead him on a little longer, letting him think that I might reconsider, but instead I feel compelled to clarify, "I'm not offended, I'm just not a prostitute."

I ponder the odds of ever again being offered money to accept head from a hot-looking foreign guy. If the probability of a given outcome to an event is P and the event is repeated N times, then the larger N becomes, so the likelihood increases that the closer, in proportion, will be the occurrence of the given outcome to N*P. In other words, how many times I win, depends on how many times I play the game.

Descartes' Ugly Mother

When I'm working on a problem, I never think about beauty.
I think only of how to solve the problem. But when I have finished, if
the solution is not beautiful, I know it is wrong.
— *R. Buckminster Fuller*

What I love about my work has less to do with number crunching and more to do with story telling. When it comes down to sorting out what happened, there are, at minimum, three sides to every story; their side, our side, and the multi-dimensional, ever-elusive truth.

As an advocate, it is my job to demonstrate our client's version of reality. A carefully crafted spin is acceptable, but under no circumstances may I falsify or twist the facts. If I did, it would risk our most valuable resource, credibility. A potential short-term gain would inevitably reap disaster over the long haul in this business.

When he develops his alternatives to the reality that the opposition lays out for us, Dan, a former boxer, imagines his role in terms of good guys and bad guys. A bare knuckles bar fight, a boxing match, a wild west shoot out, black hat or white, it doesn't make much difference which one he wears, as long as it's a good and bloody fight. When Dan prepares his rebuttal, arguing the logic or inappropriate use of a particular statistical method, behind the mathematical jargon, what he really means to say is, *Your ugly mama sucks eggs.*

Dan has a way of making even the driest of case materials seem more exciting. I'm not much of a fighter, but I have my own way of creating something meaningful to me. I like to imagine that I am painting a picture or telling a story. Nothing is ever as simple as tabulating, validating, and reporting a set of scores. We need to go back further, build a context, paint the background and develop a plot.

If we know what the end of the story needs to be, the questions we ask of the data will lead us there. We may throw in one or two MacGuffins, meaningless storylines that Hitchcock frequently applied, devices to distract and lead the observer astray. In our case, a MacGuffin is a data problem that we lead the opposition to believe our side has misused or overlooked. Should they take the bait, we are prepared to make them look foolish or overzealous in their efforts.

Dan, with his extensive knowledge of statistical theory, is more inclined to attack the analyses and cite faulty interpretations of the data. For example, he may shred their sampling methods, data management, or choice of statistical tests, often all three. As Dan attacks the validity of the arguments, I am more likely to challenge the underlying assumptions on which they are based. In philosophy, this refers to an "original position," the premise from which one builds a proposition. Seventeenth century philosopher and mathematician, Descartes, distilled the ultimate original position, Cogito ergo sum.

When Dan and I collaborate, the details may change, but the format is always the same. You asked the wrong question. You answered it incorrectly. You bastard.

A complementary, if sometimes volatile relationship, Dan and I frequently amuse each other by conjuring and developing sophisticated, mathematical arguments to disprove the existence of Descartes' not-too-choosy, unattractive, egg-sucking mother.

Immediately Double Your Chances of Finding a Date

Introductions are tricky in a lesbian relationship. It's a word game. To my friends she's my lover, to strangers and family members in denial she's my roommate, to Jehovah's Witnesses at the door she's my lesbian sex slave, and to my mother she's Jewish and that's all that matters.

— *Denise McCanles*

It is about a socialist, anti-family political movement that encourages women to leave their husbands, kill their children, practice witchcraft, destroy capitalism and become lesbians.

— *Pat Robertson*

It's not that I don't like penises, I just don't like them on men.

— *Lea DeLaria*

Tips In: $168
Tips Out: $25

Two college age women sit down together at my stage. With no sign of a man accompanying them, along with the cues of their dowdy clothing and absence of make-up, I make an educated guess at their sexual preference. As I lean down to make contact and take their tips, I ask "Are you two *real* lesbians or is this just some assignment for your sociology class?" I get the laugh that I'm looking for and they tell me that they are, in fact, real live lesbians.

Apparently they both share a crush on Micki, a heavily tattooed and pierced dancer, and are waiting for her arrival on this stage. Other than the fact that Micki is bi-sexual, I suspect her appeal has more to do with her bad girl image than anything else. She frequently appears on stage under the influence, the influence of exactly what being none of my business. She drinks, smokes, and womanizes heavily. Occasionally it is necessary to step around Micki making out

97

with a female customer she has snuck into the dressing room at the very end of the shift.

I join them at their table. Jenny and Cory live together. Jenny works for an adult cable channel, and I grill her about how someone lands a cool job like that. She knew someone, what else is new. They want me to tell them everything I know about Micki, if I know her real name (I don't), if she has a steady girlfriend (no clue).

Sincere lesbian activity is hard to discern around here. We offhandedly touch and lavish compliments on one another. I surprised myself the first time I told another girl what a great ass she had, but she gave herself a little spank and agreed with me wholeheartedly. Instead of the, "No, are you blind? I hate my...fill in the blank," as I am so used to hearing women reply whenever they are offered a compliment.

Sometimes the girls massage each other's shoulders in the dressing room, brush each other's hair, or give hugs and closed mouthed kisses. Completely relaxed and tactile in various states of undress; we are intensely sensual, but at the same time casual and completely unselfconscious. It's playful and sexy, but the boundaries and intent are unclear. I've never tried to guess at the orientations of other dancers. We're surrounded by sexual energy and visually stimulated by beautiful women in an environment where expressing any resulting impulses is richly rewarded.

That said, I've developed a small crush of my own on Lana, a dark-haired Hawaiian Tropic swimsuit-model type beauty. Since her first display of affection toward me on stage, we've been playing that game more and more often. Once, as she was leaving the stage and I was coming on, she kissed me, full on the mouth, a little tongue. I was shocked, but enjoyed it. I've been asking around about her trying to find out if she might really like me or if she is just pretending so that we get more money. Then when I hear she probably likes me, I assume I'm just being teased. One of these days I'll pass her a note in gym class to find out for sure.

When Jenny and Cory get over the fact that I have nothing to offer in the way of bringing them closer to Micki, I have all kinds of questions to ask them. Fascinating, probing questions like, why do you come here? Their answer, "To see boobs, of course!"

I thought lesbians were above all that. I guess we all have something to learn about stereotypes. Jenny and Cory come in about once every five or six weeks. Apparently, women get in free, and the two of them limit the number of drinks they order to keep it from getting too expensive an outing. I ignore the fact that they have been lousy tippers so far and continue asking stupid questions.

"Do you get excited when you come here and go home for sex?" I ask. Jenny answers for the two of them, "No, we come out to drink and see boobs."

"So, it doesn't turn you on?"

"No, not really," Cory replies as if this were an insane question.

"We love to fuck either way. Coming here is fun, but we don't need it to get going. We just like to see different sets of tits whenever we get the chance."

I ask because some nights, I can't wait to get home and climb on top of my husband. I leave the lights off, but wake him up. I'm sure I reek from the smoke and sweat, but he hasn't complained. Sometimes I get horny from watching the other dancers, but more often the prelude to our coupling is a particularly erotic private dance.

I'm pretty wired from the long drive home. It's almost an hour home even with no traffic at 2:00 AM. As I drive I have a lot of time to reminisce over the events of the evening. By the time I walk in the door, I'm wide-awake, my legs aren't so sore, and I've had hours of foreplay. He wants to hear what happened that night, and any salacious details, or exaggerated confessions I might be prepared to make.

I tend to offer private dances to men that I find attractive or at the very least, interesting to talk to, and I take pride in my ability to provide erotic pleasure. I am sincere in my work ethic and in my desire to make him want me desperately from a distance of at least fifteen inches, but I often relish it as well. I want him to be visually pleased by me. I want to seduce him without laying a hand on him. When I stare into a customer's eyes and gyrate in front of him, I enjoy being sexual, and I feel so much less inhibited than I once did. I feel more confident both inside and outside the club and more sensual at home. I move like a dancer. I feel charming, but also notorious with a dark secret.

Instead of looking at him, I watch my body in the mirror. Very different from my exuberant persona on stage, I am sultry and utterly pleased with myself. Resting on my elbows and knees with my backside in the air and my back arched deeply, I stretch each leg out behind me like a cat, very slowly and with absolute precision. I want him to use his eyes on me as he might use his hands, gently tracing the outline of my body with his slow, moving gaze instead of his fingertips. As I move about and pose in front of him, he can feel the heat radiating off my skin.

I press my back up against the mirror and reach out for my legs and draw them back in, pulling my knees against my chest and wrapping my arms tightly around them, and then relax, leaning back with my hands in my hair. He is riveted to me, but now I don't care what he thinks. I am pleasing myself, not him. Though in one way he is merely a bystander, I am not fraudulent or withholding. In the space we have carved out for ourselves in this conditionally public arena, we are sharing a private confidence, if not a truly intimate one.

He is the beneficiary of an intensely personal and rare event in which I am completely satisfied in my own body. I am beautiful and although he is my witness, for once I don't need one.

A bad girl. A biker chick. Tawdry and glamorous.

When I walk though the corridors at work, inside I feel like Blaze Starr instead of a small, bookish woman with unflattering eyeglasses and a mild speech impediment.

Mothers of Invention

One must still have chaos in oneself to give birth to a dancing star.

— Nietzsche

Tips In: $218
Tips Out: $35
Three T-Bars: $30

Every Wednesday and Saturday, Lily comes by to sell costumes. Lily is a teeny tiny Asian lady with a very loud voice. She is abrupt and barely understandable. Her caustic demeanor and heavily accented broken English makes her seem cartoonish, but this makes her no less intimidating to me. Lily makes the rounds going from dancer to dancer, club to club, rolling a garment rack of easily removed custom fitted evening gowns into the dressing rooms of all the clubs in Puget Sound.

Dancers spend a large proportion of their incomes on costumes and big shoes. She tries to bully me into buying a dress, but I've got plenty of clothes, so instead I satisfy her by rummaging through her oversized duffle bag for an assortment of T-bars. I find a gold lame', silver lame' and a funky 70s looking flower print for a total of $30.

Lydia looks for something made to order, extra long but, as usual, she has no cash. She asks if Lily will let her make payments and is surprised when Lily agrees. Lily answers her loudly, "I not worried. Dancer always pay me. One girl, she move out of town, she quit. But she start the dancing again, different club. I find her. I say, you owe me fifty-five dollar! Her mouth hang wide open like, how I find her? How I remember that? Dancer always pay me. I don't worry about it."

Pandora has disappeared. I finally ask Michael what is going on. "The redhead? She quit."

"She didn't give you any notice or say where she was going?" She didn't tell me that she was thinking of quitting.

"No, that happens a lot. Girls come and go. They just stop coming to work. Sometimes they come back, usually with a lame excuse about why they never called."

"Well how do you know she's okay? What if something has happened to her?"

"I tried calling her a couple of times, but she hasn't called back. Most of the dancers don't give any notice. They just stop coming, it's very common." Michael isn't worried. He thinks Pandora's a flake, and I guess he is probably right.

Shit. She still has a bunch of my outfits and my over-the-knee Victoria's Secret black boots. I don't know her real name, and I don't have her phone number. I go check on her locker, but someone has already claimed it. I haven't seen my costumes on anyone else so far, but I'll keep my eyes open.

This is the first time it has occurred to me that I know not one of the dancer's real names. I don't know whether she left her things behind or who to ask about it. If someone has my stuff and I ask around about it, they're likely to hide it. I'll just have to wait and see if Pandora or my costumes turn up eventually.

Moni and Samantha stumble into the dressing room. It looks as if they've spent the day getting drunk together. Moni isn't supposed to be here tonight but she is anyway, being generally obnoxious and hanging all over Samantha.

"People always tell me I look just like Winona Ryder. You don't think I look like Winona Ryder, do you?" Moni queries in my general direction.

"Maybe a little, only younger." I answer. Moni is barely eighteen and she looks more like fifteen. She's a brat who gets on my nerves. Samantha is old enough to know better, but I think she enjoys having the one-woman fan club following her around like a pet.

I imagine my own daughter in a place like this and start to wonder about these young women and what their moms might be like.

"Hey, I thought of a new question." This is a good time for my question of the night. It's still slow enough that we aren't too busy or distracted, early enough that we aren't rushing to get out of here, and it seems we would all prefer the attention drawn away from Moni and her big show of underage drunkenness.

"Does your mother know you strip?"

They all laugh, but most of the girls say yes, their mothers know.

"My mom lives in Portland. I used to tell her that I was a waitress, I'm pretty sure she believed me, but I had this asshole boyfriend who called her up and told her that I was a whore and a stripper. I probably could have convinced her that he was full of shit and was just trying to piss me off, but I went ahead and told her. She said it didn't bother her, but that I'd better be careful. She thinks someone will rape me or strangle me or something."

"I tell my mom that I bartend here. I don't know if she knows Allures is a tittie bar."

"My mom knows, but she pretends she doesn't and won't bring it up. I don't see her that much anyway."

"Oh God, my mom would freak! No way, I would never tell her anything."

Moni pulled a sequined halter top out of her bag and held it up to show us, "My mom sews most of my costumes for me."

"Wow, that's cute. So it doesn't bother her?"

"No, not at all, I mean, she wants me to be safe and all, but she thinks this club is pretty classy. I make good money and I have fun. She knows I've always wanted to be a stripper"

"Was she ever a stripper?" I ask. Any of their mom's could have been strippers, but for some reason I've never considered that before.

"Have any of your moms ever done this?" I look around. More generalized laughter.

"Oh, man, not my mom!"

"Gross! No one would pay to see that, that's for sure!"

Moni answers me, "Nah, but she would have. She doesn't see anything wrong with it. She likes to design my outfits, and I think I could even sell some of these."

Lydia asks me about my mother.

This place can make you forget you are somebody's daughter or somebody's mother for that matter. In a lot of ways, it is a good thing.

"I'm sure my mother would prefer that I keep all of this to myself." I imagine my mother with a stern, we-are-not-amused look on her face, but in her eyes a hint of begging me to say I'm just kidding and then please drop the subject. That's how I think it would go.

I can't think of a more biased person to describe a woman than her own daughter. First of all, I actually do call my mother, "Mother," not Mom or Ma or Mama. I'm the youngest, so her title was not mine to determine. Nevertheless, it fits.

The roots of my feminism come directly from my mother. When she was very young, she loved to play sandlot baseball. She said she was the second best player on the team. The one player better than her grew up to play baseball professionally. When the little league was finally organized in her town, plans for what would certainly be the best summer ever occupied her imagination. She couldn't wait to get her uniform.

That night, when her father came home from work, he sat down on her bed and quietly explained to her that she would not be part of the team, that little league was only for boys.

I could just see that little girl sitting there with her father, trying to understand, taking in that early lesson that life isn't fair. As much as I couldn't relate to any desire to play baseball, I could still feel her disappointment and confusion, and buried beneath that, her anger. I must have asked her to tell me that story a hundred times. It was like a comforting bedtime story; as if she were reassuring me, *that's what happened to me, but will never happen to you.*

I imagined myself in her place and knew that whatever it was that I wanted to do, my parents would make sure that no one and nothing would keep me from trying. Not that there was much her dad could do about it. That's just how things were, but knowing my parents were always on my side, no matter what, helped to make me a more open, secure person. If you don't root for your kids, who will?

Having expressly raised my daughter to be conscious of feminist issues, I've taught her to understand and honor her rights and freedoms, and, as she grows up, to strive toward independence. I did not want her to grow up imagining herself as only her role in relation to someone else, someone's "right arm" or the "woman behind the man", but herself, an emotionally, physically, and economically independent woman. Like my mother, that was my way of reassuring her that she can do whatever she wants in life, too.

The most defining thing I can say about my mother is that I have never seen her cry. She is an incredibly strong woman, both emotionally and physically, and has absolute, unwavering control over her feelings. Growing up, she never let me see any chinks in her armor. Well into my teens, I felt as though I could never live up to the standards she set.

Understandably, my pregnancy at seventeen thoroughly embarrassed and disappointed her. Once the first trimester had passed and it was too late for an abortion, rather than simply talk to me face to face, she began to make a habit of leaving advice column clippings about the virtues of adoption on my pillow at night. I knew she did it because she cared, but I learned to dread coming home to whatever I might find on my pillow that night.

I always knew that if I needed something, anything at all, she would provide it. It was she who could be counted on to protect and defend us against whatever might come our way, including the mundane details of family maintenance.

Until my son was born and my mother and I became closer, I never felt as though I knew the real her. My mother lived and breathed her role as our perfect mother, to the exclusion of her true self. Her version of an ideal mother, an image that seemed so important for her to convey to her children, cloaked the person I wished I had known all my life — a funny, smart, but wonderfully flawed woman. It just goes to show that even a perfect mother gets blamed for everything, including being too perfect.

Different from my mother, and maybe because of her, my father was more of a risk taker. Gregarious and outgoing, he was the fun parent. He was warm and loved to spoil in the grandest of styles at every opportunity. However, as it is with my mother, it is hard to separate the person from his role. I know what he is like as my father, but as a person, I don't think I do. All I can say is that if my mother was my roots, then he was certainly my wings.

My mother and my daughter are the two most amazing women I know. They are very much alike, strong, independent, and fiercely loyal. My daughter looks and sounds just like my mother, athletic and petite, fair, and blue-eyed with a wry wit and a deep voice. However, where my mother is stoic and reserved, my daughter is passionate and hyperbolic. Unlike my mother, she will have no trouble at all expressing her disappointment with me, if and when it comes to that. She may understand that I made a choice that was mine to make. Or she may think of me as a fraud or a failure in everything I've taught her. I don't know which of the two of them it will be harder to explain all this.

Which is worse, a stripper daughter or a stripper mother?

Good Hair Days

Of two evils, choose the prettier.

— *Carolyn Wells*

Both Delilah and Moni have always wanted to be strippers. The minute they turned eighteen, they were taking it off. Maybe it's a generational thing. They're both under twenty-one. They grew up in the Clinton era, whereas I grew up in the Reagan era. By the time they were in kindergarten, Madonna had already made nudity fairly blasé and frequently annoying. These girls have seen things in the news that I would have only seen in horror movies. Soft-core pornography is on five different cable channels every night starting at eight o'clock and yet, someone out there is still fascinated by strippers. They must be. Like clockwork, there is the ubiquitous newspaper article or TV segment about women putting themselves through nursing school or stripping for God or a single mom trying to make ends meet as an exotic dancer.

It's as though the media is desperate to hang on to that one tiny sliver of salaciousness, desperate to keep that one corner shrouded in mystery and fantasy and shame, when the rest of us simply fail to be shocked by it anymore. While we may not be shocked, as a populous, we are still deeply fascinated.

Although Delilah appears to be growing up and out of this job, it is not the dancing she dislikes, it's the strippers. Neither Delilah nor Moni, or any of the young girls it appears, are the least bit embarrassed about being strippers. As much as I've fought it, I am embarrassed. I keep thinking I'll be found out. Exposed. I'll be shopping at the mall or walking around the university and I'll see a man walking in my direction and wonder if he has seen me at the club. I keep thinking that someone is going to yell and point at me. I know it's silly, but I keep imagining that someone I don't even know will try to humiliate me in front of my children.

It's like being fourteen and seen at Kmart. If someone sees you in there, they have to be there, too, right? But it doesn't work the same way with stripping. It's somehow okay or normal for men to pay to see women take their clothes off, but it isn't okay or normal for women to take money to take their clothes off for men.

While I'm dancing, I don't feel the least bit ashamed, I feel great. I love my costumes and make up. You feel like a different person — anyone you want to be — and you can change as often as you have costumes. Lydia told me once that dancing at Zoot Allures makes her feel like a movie star.

"This is as close as I'll ever come to being a movie star. When I'm on the stage, all eyes are on me. Everyone wants to know me. I've even had guys ask for my autograph. I was so surprised that I started to write my real name! It was sweet."

I know what she means. They hand us money, buy us drinks, and follow us around. Sometimes customers bring flowers and gifts. They'll practically beg for a date. I wake up and in the mirror is my married, raggedy, thirty-four year old, remnants of last night's make-up under my puffy eyes, pasty face and I smile, reminiscing about the well-dressed young man who pleaded with me last night for a date.

It makes me feel good.

The clothes and the make up and the lighting makes us look as though we are thinner and have much better complexions than we really do. Some of the dancers like to wear wigs. Melanie has a shiny black wig that she wore the first time I saw her. The wig is chin length with bangs cut straight across. It's very sophisticated and gives her a dramatic departure from her longer, naturally blonde hair. Her voluptuous body is unmistakable, even below a Cleopatra wig. I guess we all need a break from our established personas from time to time. Miranda will sometimes pull her long, red hair into a tight bun and customers will offer to pay her to let it down. Sometimes she is rude and nasty to customers only to have them pay her even more for her attention. She strides into the dressing room waving twenties at the rest of us, "This is what I get for being a total bitch!"

Unlike Melanie who changes only her wig between sets, Sunny, another natural blonde, arrives at the club wearing a dark wig bringing with her a different character and stage name. I've only met Sunny a couple times and I've never actually seen Diandra. Marcus is the one who told me about Diandra, this dancer within a dancer.

"Diandra is Sunny's alter-ego, her dark side, her evil twin." Marcus gets very animated as he talks about her. I think he might have a crush on Sunny. I don't remember what brought her up, but I'm pretty sure I didn't ask.

"Did you know that Sunny's parents are hippies and that her real name is Rainbow?"

"Rainbow?"

"Rainbow."

Even if you only go from Rainbow to Sunny, a definite plus of this job is the option to start fresh any time you want.

Handsome, Professional SWM ISO F, Extroverts Preferred...

Top 10 things likely to be overheard from a Klingon Programmer

    10. Specifications are for the weak and timid!

    9. You question the worthiness of my code? I should kill you where you stand!

    8. Indentation?! I will show you how to indent when I indent your skull!

    7. What is this talk of *release*? Klingons do not make software *releases*. Our software *escapes* leaving a bloody trail of designers and quality assurance people in its wake.

    6. Klingon function calls do not have *parameters* - they have arguments - and they always win them.

    5. Debugging? Klingons do not debug. Our software does not coddle the weak.

    4. A true Klingon Warrior does not comment on his code!

    3. Klingon software does NOT have bugs. It has features, and those features are too sophisticated for a Romulan pig like you to understand.

    2. You cannot truly appreciate Dilbert unless you've read it in the original Klingon.

    1. Our users will know fear and cower before our software! Ship it! Ship it and let them flee like the dogs they are!

Tips In: $119
Tips Out: $25

I don't understand why they want to date us. Even though I almost always admit that I'm married, I still get asked out at least every other shift.

"We are strippers. We show them our tits for dollar bills. Why on earth do they insist on inviting us to dinner? Can you explain this to me?" I say to no one in particular, but Emotion answers me,

"Why not? What do you think is wrong with us? We're hot and sexy, and they can talk to us. Why are you always so down on yourself? Of course they want to go out with you." She's pissed at me. She thinks I'm putting us down.

"I didn't mean it that way. I just don't understand why they don't try to meet regular girls. Don't you think that if you said yes, they'd be scared shitless?

"Well, maybe that's why they ask."

I have my own small following. Delilah was right, it didn't take very long. Computer geeks tend to gravitate toward me. I keep them coming back usually by talking about software and programming. It blows their minds, I can actually *see* them falling in love with me as they realize that I am their dream girl, the one they've been looking for all this time. A big-titted, half-naked woman who roots for the Linux open source model to someday supersede Windows. A woman who understands why they feel compelled to write and re-write programs using fewer and fewer lines of code, but that will still run. A woman who knows what the T. in James T. Kirk stands for. Where have I been all his life? So they're thinking, she could blow me, make me a sandwich, and later, help me debug this program. That's almost as good as having a flat head for him to rest a beer can on. Okay, that's not really very fair of me. In fact, most of them seem very sincere.

There is one young man, Stephen, who has been coming to see me regularly every Monday night. He says he likes to come in on the slow night so he doesn't have to share me, not too much anyway. There isn't much to do on Monday nights, and he is fun to talk to. He's a project manager with a global telecommunications company headquartered in Tacoma. Where were all these young men with good jobs when I was single?

I've told him that I'm married, but it doesn't seem to matter. He brings me a single red rose every time he comes in. There is no vase for me to put them in, and the air quality in the building is so bad that the roses start to wilt and dry up by the end of my shift at 2:00 AM, but it doesn't make it any less sweet. Since he's been coming in so reliably, I've been asking him to order a dinner for Lydia first thing each time he comes in. This way I know she gets at least one meal (such as it is) on a regular basis. I think he likes being needed just the same as I do.

"Do you think we could go out to lunch sometime?"

"Maybe sometime." Delilah told me it is better to be vague than to reject anyone outright.

"Well, how about Wednesday?"

"No, I can't make it Wednesday. You remember I'm married, right?"

"It's just lunch."

"Well, I don't believe my husband would think so. Give me some time to think about it, okay?"

"Okay."

Stephen has hung around longer than any of my other regulars, but he'll get tired of me eventually and move on to someone else.

Career Trajectories

Not everything that can be counted counts, and not everything that counts can be counted.

— Albert Einstein

We have an old gender discrimination case that was settled quite a while back, but our firm still handles the clients continued compliance. It was regional retail store that was accused of not promoting female employees to management positions in rates equal to that of male employees. The company had attempted to defend itself by arguing that the appropriate chain of advancement in their company began with the entry-level position of "Night Stocker".

The reason fewer women made it up the ranks was due to their lack of interest in stocking items at night. They were much more likely to be cashiers, and as any fool knows, being a night stocker provides many more of the skills and experience needed to be a good manager. Plus, a willingness to work nights highlights a personal commitment to the company.

This case had been settled long before I got here so I had no particular feeling about it one way or the other; nevertheless, it is obvious that their promotion practices were not highly defensible. Ultimately, they settled and as far as I know, are doing what they need to do to change the hiring practices that, whether intended or not, had an unfair impact on women in their company.

This afternoon, as Lynne made her rounds, she stopped by in order to point out that my plants appear to be dying. I happened to be reading recent updates to the case file, and I made a comment about that particular case and the transparent bias of their hiring practices.

"I personally interviewed employees of that chain. The women chose to be cashiers. They knew managers were hired from the pool of night stock persons. This company did nothing discriminatory. Never, ever read the reports of plaintiff and assume they reflect the truth. I don't care if it is a private comment to me, don't ever make a statement that undermines our client again."

The case had already been settled; otherwise I might understand her vehemence as she spoke to me.   One would not want to potentially undermine any case by expressing an offhand contrary opinion, but this was incredible.   The client didn't continue to retain our services just because they enjoyed mailing us checks.   They still had plenty for us to do.   I sat there with my mouth hanging open for just a second, then nodded to express that I understood her as she sashayed out of my office.

I tended to my plants, wilting in here just like me.   And I paced for a while, then stared out my big window at all the other office buildings, trying to see the people inside, but I couldn't.

It is one thing to *say* that your client is innocent, quite another to believe it.

Bad Girls

Do what you feel in your heart to be right - for you'll be criticized anyway. You'll be damned if you do, and damned if you don't.
— *Eleanor Roosevelt*

Tips In: $195
Tips Out: $30

The greatest advice I ever got was from a stripper. I'm waiting to go on Stage Four in the smoking lounge. Melanie is almost done. I guess I am a little too early or something because I get the sense she is annoyed with me. Maybe I'm crowding her. Before she says anything to me, I apologize, from her point of view, out of nowhere, because I assume I must be doing something wrong. She takes my hand as we switch places.

"Babe, you have to stop thinking you're doing something wrong. Let me explain my philosophy to you."

"Yes?"

"Do whatever it is you need to do until somebody tells you to stop." Melanie's credo gives rise to an interesting question of the day (night).

"What is the worst thing you get away with?"

I'm not sure how much I will get out of them on this. With this many girls in the back, at least one is probably a snitch for Michael.

"What do you mean?" Roxy asks.

"Well, ok, I've read all the rules, but if I followed every single one of them, I'd never make any money."

"No shit. This place is barely PG—13. We can't do shit."

"What do you mean, what do I get away with?" Anabelle asks.

"She means like when I am doing a private dance, and I pull my T-bar over a little and give them a peek," Micki says.

"Oh. Well, yeah, if they are handing over twenty after twenty, I'm inclined to show a little more."

Miranda explains, "You can usually get away with brushing your tits against them, but make sure you get the extra money first or they might cum in their pants. Once they do that, they won't give you any more."

"Ahh, duly noted."

Micki adds her two cents, "For a hundred, I'll let them stick a finger in, but only if I'm sure no one can see me. If anyone does see you, they'll just ask for some of the money you got for doing it, it's not that big of a deal. The bouncers never rat you off, they just want more money, but other dancers might do it just to fuck you over. Even still, you'd probably just get a lecture, then just don't do it for a few weeks."

"What about all those cameras? I heard that Michael reviews the tapes every night," Anabelle says.

"Marcus told me there isn't even any film in them."

I jump in. "God, I hope not. It would be pretty expensive unless you tape over it once in a while. He probably sells the tapes of us to someone who puts it on the internet. He's probably making millions selling video of the shit he tells us we can't do!"

"I think there is tape in them." Emotion, in her typically honest, straight to the point way, seems to crystallize what most, if not all of us have been through. She tells us, "Either way, when I started dancing, I did all kinds of things that I knew I shouldn't because I didn't know any better. I guess I was trying to please everybody. I let them get away with too much because I thought I ought to. I didn't think I was good enough to say no. Now I have limits and I stick to them, even if it means I don't make that extra few dollars. It's not worth it to me."

"I know what you mean. I've done things that I would definitely be embarrassed about if I saw them later on tape," I admit and hope someone else admits it, too, so I don't feel so stupid. I have to settle for nods of agreement. I still worry about those tapes popping up on the internet somewhere.

I have been playing this by ear. I didn't set limits on what I would and would not do in any given situation because I didn't have any clue what I might get myself into. One private dance in particular comes to mind.

It's an off night, but I am still doing well thanks to one generous customer. He likes my long, curly hair and keeps reaching out to touch it. Once again, there isn't anything obviously wrong with this customer. I'm sure he could meet and enjoy sex with a real woman if he tried half as hard as he's trying with me. He looks a little like a biker, but not at all scary, in fact, he's just about as sweet as he could be following me around like a puppy. He has long frizzy hair pulled back into a ponytail and a thick beard. He wants a private dance and because it is so slow, there is no one else at the table dance area. He starts with forty dollars for two songs. I don't know why this is, but even now when a man spends money I feel like I owe it to him to bend the rules a little. It's not like I need the money, I just feel funny taking it without doing something extra in return. I don't want to hurt his feelings.

I whisper filthy things in his ear.

"Do you want to put your hands on me?" I barely hear him say yes.

"Do you want me?"

"Oh God, yes"

"I'll bet you do" He hands me another twenty and gets suddenly much braver.

"Let me see your pussy."

He follows my hands with his eyes as I run my fingers over my belly and down the inside of my thigh. He leans in close to me and whispers, "Please, please let me see it."

"You know I can't do that. I'll get in trouble." He looks around, "No one will know. I won't tell anyone, I promise."

"No, I can't."

He can tell I'm wavering, so he opens his wallet again. Now I have sixty dollars, not including the money he gave me while I was on stage. I feel like I should. I want to refuse the money, but that is not what strippers do. What could it hurt for me to just show him a little?

I whisper again, "You really want me to? I don't know if I should." I can see the bulge in his pants get bigger, and he adjusts himself without taking his eyes off me for a second. I'm on my knees in front of him and I lean back, knees apart. I look around to see if anyone is watching. They are, but not too carefully. I pull the inconsequential fabric of my T-bar open just a little, and he lets out an audible sigh. I do it a few more times as I change poses in front of him, letting my hand go places I know they are not supposed to. I turn around on my knees with my bottom up in the air just a few inches away from his face. He doesn't try to touch me, so if anyone is watching us, they probably aren't too concerned yet. I turn around and lean close to him.

"I bet you are dying to fuck me."

"Oh baby, I'd make love to you for hours. Come home with me tonight."

I smile, but I don't bother responding to it.

"No, really. You wouldn't have to do anything, just let me touch you and kiss you all night. We could do more if you wanted to, but you wouldn't have to. I have money." He opens his wallet stuffed with twenties.

"I have a thousand dollars, you could have it, just come home with me. We'll have such a good time."

"No, no no. You know I can't do that. You're sweet to offer, but I don't do that. I'm married."

"You could bring your husband with you to make sure you're safe. Call him and ask him." I giggled. Now that would be an unforgettable phone call. My worry is that he would say "A thousand? Go ahead!" and I simply do not want to know that about my husband.

It's ironic that I could get into trouble for showing my vagina because rumor has it that the club will soon go bottomless. State laws prohibit mixing total nudity with alcohol, so to go bottomless they will have to make part of the club dry. I'm told that the architects' plans to turn the smoking lounge into the dry, total nude area with a separate entrance have already been drawn up.

There has been a lot of talk in the back room about it. Some of the dancers say they won't do it, and from what I hear we will be able to choose which side of the house we will work on. I'm not so sure it's really a choice. We'll have to wait and see. The dancers are afraid that all the real tips will go over there and whoever isn't willing to "show pink" might as well quit because she won't make any money.

As it is, Roxy won't even take her dance pants off to show her T-bar, so we know she won't take it all off. I'm sure Anabelle won't either. I don't know how I feel about it. Most of the rest of us haven't decided. Chances are, given the typical turnover, few of us will have to decide. I understand that for some of us it's a line that we don't cross, the divider between stripper and skank. To me, as a matter of body parts, I'm not sure what difference it makes, but that's not really the point.

The rules, as they are now... well, I don't like being told that I can't show what I want, when I want. But I like even less the idea of being coerced by finances into showing everything whether I want to or not. But I forget, *I* don't have to do anything; I can't honestly say the same for the rest of us.

"You know, I'm going to need to get back on stage soon, you don't want to waste these last few minutes talking, do you?" He stopped pushing and gave me a few more dollars during my next stage set later that night, but I never did see him again.

Later that night one of the bouncers came over to let me know that he'd seen me getting a little too friendly. I told him about the offer.

"You know if you ever want to go ahead and do it, I'll come with you and make sure you're safe. You could give me ten percent. I think that's fair."

"Have you done that before?"

"Yeah, a few times. I've never had any problems" Funny, no one mentioned that among the worst things they get away with.

"Did you go along with someone who still works here?"

"I'd never tell."

"I guess that's good to know. I'll let you know if I change my mind."

A Brief Intermission

That would be a good thing for them to cut on my tombstone: Wherever she went, including here, it was against her better judgment.

— *Dorothy Parker*

I went through an academic library database to review what scholars had written recently about stripping. I found a dissertation that looks worthwhile, but the author was a customer, not a dancer.

A former stripper wrote several pieces that I found very interesting, but she writes under the auspices of an organization that seeks to abolish strip clubs. The author, Kelly Holsopple, is co-founder of the Metropolitan Coalition Against Prostitution in Minneapolis, Minnesota. I can't disagree with a lot of what the author reports, but she includes only the perspectives that support that agenda - dancers are exploited, degraded and de-humanized. In her introduction to "Strip clubs according to strippers: Exposing workplace sexual violence," (1998) she writes that she "investigates women's experiences from the women's point of view." I respectfully disagree.

Holsopple describes the dancer's experiences as if these women are empty-headed children with no agency, no free will, with no minds of their own. It's true, sometimes these aren't really choices, but decisions made between rocks and hard places. I argue that working in a poorly run strip club isn't any worse or different from working in a job you despise, or remaining in a lousy marriage year after year, simply because you don't know what else to do.

Two articles stand out for their sensitive, yet accurate depictions of what goes on in strip clubs. "Turn-ons for money" by Carol Rambo Ronai and Carolyn Ellis (1989) is an ethnography written by a woman who stripped while she worked on her Master's thesis. The article describes the interactions between dancers and customers, and the strategies employed to build a relationship that has too often been oversimplified by the phrase "counterfeit intimacy" (Foote, 1954). The first author's methods were very similar to mine, collecting

123

information as a participant observer, but with a much more directed academic purpose of documenting and interpreting these distinct social interactions. I may have convinced myself that science was my purpose as well, but I don't believe that anymore.

"The occupational milieu of the exotic dancer" by Craig Forsyth and Tina Deshotels (1997) is the journal article I both love and hate the most. This is an interview-based, descriptive article about the occupation of topless dancing. It focuses on the labor of people who work in strip clubs, including the behaviors and interactions among all the people inside the strip clubs — dancers, customers, wait staff, bartenders, bouncers, DJs, managers — everyone. I love it because it clings to one central assumption; stripping isn't a crime, it's a job. I hate it because it was published in a journal in the social sciences descriptively named, "Deviant Behavior."

I find it absurd that an activity, one that has been around for so long, is legal, and is such a mainstream part of our culture, at least for those of us who know the joys of cable TV, is still classified as deviant. To me, on-line chat rooms are deviant. Deviance must be in the eye of the beholder.

Men are visual creatures. Women can make a living providing visual stimulation to men who have the means and are willing to pay for it. The existence of strip clubs may very well be unhealthy and seedy, a product of collective sexual repression and individual below-par childhoods, double standards and employment discrimination, but I take issue with assigning the label of deviant onto strippers. At various stages of life, as in the context of bachelor parties, private social clubs, or fraternity hazing, men engage in a wide range of activities that may be stupid or childish, but are not considered deviant, and ultimately, are socially accepted and occasionally even lionized.

It's a cop out to stereotype the motivations of a stripper and ignore their place among an entire industry and its patrons. These women aren't out on the street dancing around and taking their clothes off for no one in particular. Nor are they privately exchanging sexual favors for cash. In strip clubs, respectable, hard-working men show up to the party. The trade revolves around money and power, and maybe even a sense of glamour and excitement that is hard to come by nowadays.

124

The exchange and the duality of the strip club experience is somehow stylish and cosmopolitan, and at the same time, repulsive and pathetic.

Thanks to the internet, the market for visual stimulation and fantasy appears to be both expanding and insatiable. Beyond this oversimplification, people are lonely. Maybe some men are both lonely and too damn lazy to obtain and maintain a real relationship with a real woman, so they go grab a fantasy for an evening.

Some are regulars, their stripper girlfriend makes them feel special and sexy, and isn't around to make life complicated during the week. Do I feel sorry for these men? Sure, but I don't think they are deviant or even necessarily dysfunctional. They want to create a fantasy about who they are, not just about who I am.

He wants to feel powerful and desired. He wants to compete with other men for my attention and win. He wants to be my white knight or my dangerous gangster boyfriend. I am a victim of sad, dramatic circumstances beyond my control and although right now I'm working as a stripper, I don't belong here and he will save me. Who knew he was paying attention when Pretty Woman kept popping up on HBO? I'm a virgin. I have a heart of gold. I'm putting myself through college. My stepfather tried to molest me, so I ran away and ended up here.

Customers especially love this one because it implies that sexual advances were successfully fended off. They want to believe that who they see before them is the untouched, untamed, fighter of a girl doing what she has to do to get by, as opposed to the much more likely scenario that she was abused for years, became promiscuous, and maybe even drug-addicted, before finally getting loose. At least in the former scenario, customers are potential rescuers and not personally complicit in a perpetual cycle of exploitation, that is, if one views it as exploitation. Either way, they can forget that without them, there would be no market for a sex industry.

I have sheer contempt for the double standards that exist in these warped, sexualized social arenas, but I have to accept what is and not keep trying to shift my attention to what ought to be. Maybe women ought not sell their bodies and maybe men ought not buy them, but they do and the transactions occur in a society that has differential norms, expectations, and reward systems by gender.

125

One can take issue with my choice of words, selling bodies, selling sexual entertainment, buying power over another human being, however one may define it, an aspect of human sexuality is transformed into a commodity. One may argue with my position that gender relations, in general, are lopsided, however, I believe that in both the public and private spheres — legal, social, economic, political, and physical — women tend to be at a systematic disadvantage.

If you don't believe me, check out the Bureau of Labor Statistics website, or the gender composition of all three branches of government, or the demographics of the prison population versus that of typical crime victims. I don't call it a male conspiracy, or wish that some bureaucratic agency could or ought to intervene on behalf of all women, just that it is, and that I need to accept it as the backdrop for my experience or be prepared to keep banging my head against a wall.

Freaks & Geeks

Once you can accept the universe as matter expanding into nothing that is something, wearing stripes with plaid comes easy.

— Albert Einstein

Tips In: $105
Tips Out: $25

Micki steps into the dressing room.

"Your boyfriend is here."

"Me?"

"Yeah, that dork who always comes to see you. He wouldn't let me come near him. He asked me to tell you that he is out there. It looks like he has a present for you."

"Shit. It's Saturday. He doesn't come on Saturdays. He's going to keep me from making any money tonight." I don't want to have him sit out there waiting for me, but I am not really in the mood for him either. I go to see what he wants.

"Hey there sweetie, what are you doing here tonight?"

"I brought you a present."

"You didn't have to do that. Really, you shouldn't have."

"I saw it, and I wanted to see it on you." He hands me a light blue pouch with a drawstring top. Inside was that little blue box, the kind that says Tiffany's, you know, the kind that I've never opened before. Please, please let this be something simple and relatively inexpensive, I silently plead.

"Stephen, I can't accept this. Really. It's so sweet of you, and of course, I appreciate it, but I don't think it is appropriate."

"Open the card first."

I open it. It's a lovely, romantic card with a red and magenta tissue paper heart crafted on the cover. Inside he wrote the date and, "Cheryl, To us. My love always, Stephen."

"Open the present. I can't wait. Just open it. Go ahead, I think you'll like it." I think he came in on a Saturday night to make sure a lot of people see the present he brought me.

"Okay." Inside the box is a wishbone pendant on a platinum chain. The wishbone part covered in diamonds. Oh fuck. Fuck! Fuck! What the fuck am I going to do about this!

"I know you're a vegetarian, but the wishbone signifies our wish to be together."

Oh shit. I didn't think it was a bad idea to get him to buy Lydia food. I did not think it was a bad idea to keep him hanging around, we do this all the time. This happens all the time. Do not panic.

"Oh, this is so sweet, but I really cannot accept it, it is much too much."

"I wouldn't have bought it for you if I didn't want to see it on you. Just put it on and let me see how it looks." He tries to put it on me.

"No, really. It is very sweet. Let's talk about this." I put the box back in the pouch and the pouch back in his hand.

"Okay. I'll hold onto it for now, but I know you will change your mind."

"You are such a sweet person and if I weren't married, I would certainly go out with you."

"You'd go out with me? Just go out with me?"

"You know what I mean. It's not that I don't find you attractive. We have a lot in common, but you do know that I am married, and I am also much older than you are."

"That doesn't matter. It's not even that much of a difference." He says.

I'm losing my patience. It's not like I have a whole lot of experience trying to brush someone off, much less turning down diamond jewelry. I don't want to hurt his feelings, he means well. Maybe I should just accept the gift and say, yes, to whatever he plans, then blow him off.

He stays until closing tonight. It makes it very hard to dance on stage and impossible to sell a private dance. I go home with the card, but insist he hold on to the jewelry, telling him that I would have no way to explain it to my husband, which is true.

Monday morning I couldn't help myself. I look the pendant up on the Tiffany & Co. website. It retails for $1,950. That is more than twice as much as my husband paid for my wedding ring. I still have the card in my purse, and I pull it out to look at it again, not because I feel sentimental or because I was considering his advances, I need to check something.

"Cheryl, To us. My love always, Stephen"

Cheryl? I am absolutely positive that I never told him anything other than my stage name. The only one still at the club who has even a remote chance of remembering my real name is Delilah, but I sincerely doubt it. And even if she did remember it, I don't think she'd tell him. Maybe a bouncer looked it up for him. I have no idea what kind of records they keep.

Up until now, these conflicts between my day and night jobs have remained within the confines of my head. Okay, I need to think. So he knows my real name, so what? I was crystal clear in my objections and I did not accept the gift. The next time I see him I will be firm and lay down the law.

Pandora's Locker

In Greek mythology, Pandora is the first woman on earth. Zeus ordered Hephaestus to create her as vengeance upon man and his benefactor, Prometheus. The gods endowed her with every charm, together with curiosity and deceit. Zeus sent her as a wife to Epimetheus, Prometheus' simple brother, and gave her a box that he forbade her to open. Despite Prometheus' warnings, Epimetheus allowed her to open the box and let out all the evils that have since afflicted man. Hope alone remained inside the box.

Tips In: $266
Tips Out: $40

It's a Monday night, I go on at 8:00 but I get there around 7:00. I sit in back and talk to the dancers. There is a new dancer who goes by the name of Kara. She is very tall, graceful, and lovely, with amazing green eyes. She's from Portland. Hope is there and so are Emotion and Talia. Hope is about 5'5" with reddish brown hair and fair skin, blue eyes, and a certain transparency about her that makes her look somehow threadbare. I ask my question of the night.

"What are you going to do when you're done doing this? Realistic or not." Talia wants to buy a ranch. Kara wants to be a middle school teacher. She had been a teacher's aid back in high school. Her fantasy is to be a racecar driver. Just a few Sundays ago, racing legend, Dale Earnhardt, died on the track.

Kara said, "Hey, he was happy, doing what he wanted to be doing, just like me." The others leave and I ask Hope who tells me that she, too, would like to be a teacher but that, in her words, she is mentally unstable.

"Mentally unstable? You don't seem mentally unstable to me."

"I have trouble controlling my anger. I don't even know if I can hold on to this job." She launches in, "Have you ever heard of self-mutilation? I lost my last job because someone pissed me off and I went into the bathroom and cut my arm with a box cutter. I had to go to emergency and get stitches and they fired me." She shows me the

131

big red scar along the inside of her upper arm. She begins to tell me what had been the basic themes of the past nineteen years. Sexual abuse, physical abuse, abandonment, homelessness, if it's been on daytime TV, she's been there.

"I'm just so sad all the time."

I'm sitting there thinking, *No shit*.

We talk for a while about depression. I dump out my purse and show her the various pharmaceuticals that make for better living in my home, but she is afraid of pills and of therapists. I tell her that my family care physician prescribed Paxil for my depression without me having to lie down on a couch (not that I haven't done that, too) and for the most part I'm much happier. Okay, maybe not happier, but not suicidal. Better, at least, except for the sleepiness and a recent inability to achieve orgasm — why am I giving this girl advice?

At the height of my insensitivity, it dawns on me that I am presumptuous and pushy about her seeing someone for depression. Not to mention stupid and naïve — family care physician? Gosh, Cheryl, do you think she has a family doctor? These women are constantly in and out of the emergency room for one thing or another, but check-ups are typically absent from their yearly calendars.

Her absolute vulnerability to me and to anyone else capable of sensing it left a pit in my stomach. I was sad and sorry and angry all at once and I just wanted to scoop her up and somehow fix it all and wipe it away and give her a normal young woman's life. In my delusion of objectivity, a housewife play-acting at being a stripper, I was yet another person to use this child for my own purposes. She's not telling me this so I can add it to my book. I don't know why she is telling me this.

"Hope, do you remember what Emotion said about strippers, and how one way or another, somewhere along the way they've been fucked up?" She nods affirmatively in my direction.

"When I was thirteen, my uncle tried to have sex with me."

"Yeah?" She sounds excited and almost happy to hear this.

"Well, did you let him?"

"No, but after that I got pretty slutty. I never told anyone about it until a few years ago. My parents were divorced and my father was dating this woman with two teenage daughters. I found out that my uncle was coming to visit, and I felt like I had to do something to protect them. It wasn't like I thought he might rape them, but these girls seemed innocent enough that if he got them high and made them think he was cool, you know how it is."

"Yeah, I know what you mean."

"So I went to my therapist, and she convinced me that I should tell their mother what happened so that she could protect her daughters. So I did, but I asked her please, *please,* don't tell my father. If he lived to be a hundred, he did not need to know this about his brother. So what does she do?"

"Oh shit."

"Right, at the first opportunity, she tells my dad all about it. So then I have to face him and deal with this. The thing is, I never wanted to know how he would react. Well, I never wanted to know for sure what I think I always knew. He wouldn't react at all. I'm not even sure he believed me. We swept it right back under the rug."

"What did you want him to do? Beat the shit out of your uncle?" Hope asks me this with a reverence that makes me laugh and it breaks up the tension, which is good because girls are starting to walk back in here.

"No, no. I just didn't want to know for certain that he wouldn't do anything. I spare her kids from having to deal with crap like this, and look what I get for my trouble."

"Yeah, that sucks."

"I'm okay. It wasn't all that big of a deal. I just wanted to tell you. See, I don't have my shit together either, but we'll figure this all out. You just got to keep moving, right?"

"My dad wasn't around. My mom's prick boyfriend started fucking me while she went to work to support his lazy ass. Shit, you didn't hear my turn get called, did you?"

"We'd better get out there. Let's get you a soda and something to eat." I can't help it; I'm a Jewish mother. Everything makes more sense on a full stomach.

I realize that I'm struggling because I don't want to see them, us, this way. I want to imagine them as above the bullshit rhetoric of a stripper profile. I want to see these women as powerful agents of their own lives, not emancipated infants with nowhere else to go. I am desperate to frame them as heroes of their own stories unfolding, instead of as the victims some of them are. And I just don't know what to do with this. I would not want to take away her ability to make a living or the choice to do with her body as she pleases. This is the hand Hope was dealt, and who the hell are feminist academics to tell her she can't play it? But still, I know in my heart that this is yet another bad life choice that will not be the last one for her.

If I call her exploited, I take away her agency. Am I willing to say that she is incapable of making choices for herself? Is it up to her to choose not to be a sex object? Is it up to her to take a stand for women everywhere and say, "I will no longer be exploited," when exploitation is the only thing she has ever been able to count on?

Do I even believe she is capable of imagining a place where she would not be exploited? So I guess I need to know, what's in it for her? Should she take one for the team and quit? Go work at Wal-Mart twice as many hours for minimum wage? I don't know whether she would be better off or not. And if every stripper in the world went on strike, would it make a difference? Would it make women less exploited? I don't' know, I really don't. But my gut tells me, not a snowball's chance.

This entry has put me in a mood. First, a good mood, because the stomachache this has given me suggests that I am where I need to be. I am questioning my fundamental beliefs about the world, and, however discomforting, I tend to see that as a good thing. And now a bad mood because I feel overwhelmed with thoughts about this. I can't type fast enough or find the right words to convey the many layers of this stinky onion.

The Last Dance

Success and failure are both difficult to endure.
Along with success come drugs, divorce, fornication, bullying, travel,
meditation, medication, depression, neurosis and suicide.
With failure comes failure.

— *Joseph Heller*

Today just before noon, two dozen red roses are delivered to my office. The card reads simply, "Stephen." If his goal is to frighten me, it works. Now he knows my real name and exactly where I work. What am I supposed to do now? Should I tell my husband? Michael? What can either of them do about it? He could show up here any time. Am I supposed to feel threatened? He knows where I am, but I have no idea how to get a hold of him. Even though I dread having to deal with this, I hope he shows up tonight so we can talk.

Not just the crazy, stalking customer thing, my whole life feels overwhelming. Overall, misery reigns.

Dmitri is involved in a group project at school, a submission to a regional competition for "World History Day". I'm not sure what that means, but he's been working long hours after school and on weekends with two other students and their teacher on a video for their entry. With the commute back and forth, I've barely seen my kid all month.

Last night, Allan went to pick him up at his teacher's house around ten, and as soon as they got home, Dmitri went straight to bed. The phone rang and it was Mr. Levine, the History teacher. He tells me that if Dmitri isn't prepared to come back and work all night, he is going to give him an F on the project.

"So what you are telling me is that after spending all month outside of school, nights, and weekends working on what I understand to be an extracurricular project, if he doesn't come back and spend the night with you, you are going to fail him?"

"Dmitri committed to this project. We have a tight deadline and we are nowhere near finished…"

135

"Are you out of your mind?" I should have hung up, but I could not resist the opportunity to take my generalized anger and frustration out on someone both so deserving and so willing to place himself in my path. I yelled at him.

"I don't know you, all I know is that it's getting late and my son needs to get some sleep. Some strange man is calling my house insisting that my son spend the night with him, and threatening to fail him if he doesn't."

Sensing obscenities on the horizon, Allan tried to snatch the phone from me, hoping to intervene on this man's behalf, and calm things down before I got Dmitri kicked out of school, but I wouldn't let go. I took a breath and let Mr. Levine finish his sentence.

"You know that isn't what I mean. Dmitri has a responsibility here. He just left in the middle of shooting."

"Your management skills are not my problem. He is already in bed and that is where he is going to stay. I suggest that you discuss this tomorrow with Dmitri and the school principal. If I hear anything more about my son being asked to spend the night with you, I will call the police." Satisfied that I had gotten in the last word, I hung up.

I worked very late yesterday and had to come home to *that*, then get up and go in to dance the day shift today. Exhausted and starving, I dragged myself home just a bit before 9 pm. There was nothing in the kitchen for me to eat. Apparently my family had gone out to dinner without me and didn't think to pick up anything for me to eat. That's okay, I'm getting used to my 'sourdough-toast-and-glass-of-wine-before-I-collapse' dinner.

I made my way through the unpacked boxes and junk strewn around the otherwise blank slate of our temporary lodgings to our bedroom. My husband was reading the newspaper (sadly, not the classifieds) in bed and the TV was on. I crawled in and whined for him to please, *please* rub my legs, to which he had the unmitigated nerve to respond, "No, I cleaned the kitchen."

If you are or ever have been married, you probably require no further explanation, but for the benefit of those who have not experienced this truly inexplicable artifact of the marital world of exchange, I will do my best to elucidate. In this critical moment, my loving husband truly believed that his one-time, half-assed cleaning of the kitchen, that he dirtied in the first place, was more than equivalent to me holding down two jobs. Rubbing my swollen, throbbing legs instead of reading the paper for five minutes was simply far too much to ask.

In his defense, this is not at all like him. He is one of the most loving, giving, and warmest people on this planet. On an intellectual level, I understood that the situation was making us feel out of control, and we were taking it out on each other. Nevertheless, if I could have mustered the energy, I would have lifted a chair and broken it over his head, battering him into loss of consciousness. Instead, I sighed deeply and rolled over. Enough was enough. It was time to give Zoot Allures my two weeks notice.

Meanwhile, I'd much rather give my notice to the Daughters of Phorcys and Ceto. Lately, petty office skirmishes seem bigger than life to me, and I can't seem to stop dwelling on them, probably because I am so terribly worn down. Now and then I catch Mary Beth, that bland toady earning twice what I do, saying rude things about me. Part of me knows that it is only because she feels threatened, but it still makes me crazy. I've tried to make friends, but I can't seem to find any common ground. It is true that I have not had all that many jobs, but before now making friends at work has never been a problem.

The only time I can remember Lynne or Mary Beth being friendly to me was when they overheard me on the phone arguing with Dan. I walked to Mary Beth's office where Lynne was stationed to clarify the instructions Dan had just given me. Mary Beth, who never says two words to me, actually patted the empty chair, inviting me to sit down and tell them all about how Dan was mistreating me. I declined, citing the rush I was in to get the project started, but at least I knew then how to increase my popularity around here.

Right before Thanksgiving, when my kids were still finishing up the school semester in Tucson, I caught Mary Beth ragging on me. She was standing in Jane's doorway and I stood right behind her for roughly a minute and a half. She was complaining that Lynne had allowed me a few days off to go home to my kids over the holiday.

Jane gave Mary Beth no indication that I was standing there. She let her prattle on as I stood behind her with a big stupid grin on my face, waiting to say happy holidays before I left for the airport. Note to self — Jane's not a very good friend even if I could count her among mine. Mary Beth turned to see me standing there, immediately and frantically trying to discern how much I may have heard. In fact, very little, I probably wouldn't have even realized that I was the object of her derision had she not become so flustered. Her eyes got wide, and she began talking very fast, walking me back down the hall, asking me questions about my holiday plans.

Every day is just like Christmas around here.

Planning My Big Exit

Oh, I've been stripped of my emotion
Stripped of my illusion
Equipped for locomotion
Been a party to collusion
Dancing for the fickle crowd's insane
Prancing for a nickel, like a monkey on a chain

They say that joking apart, "Dying's an art!"
It takes a lifetime to perfect it
You come on with a smile and a song
To find out that it's all going wrong
But with your head in the air as if you don't have a care
So that no one will suspect it
Just be certain when you want the curtain down
And start planning your big exit

Oh, I've been stripped of my defenses
Stripped of my composure
I've paid the consequences
And I'm Dying of exposure
Weighing up my life won't heal the wounds
of paying for the piper when I couldn't stand his tunes
You know, compared to today, Dying's okay
And we'd do better to respect it
Quality of life brings special things
But will the squalid little death swing angel's wings
If there's a Heaven on Earth, I guess I got what I'm worth
And I'm ready to accept it
I'm not certain I want the curtain down

> — *Planning My Big Exit from the musical "The Stripper"*
> *Lyricist: Richard O'Brien, Book by Alan Yates*

139

Tips In: $134
Tips Out: $25

I hate quitting. I hate quitting any job, but I especially hate quitting this job. I like it here. I fit in. I do a good job. I'm the stripper with the great attitude. I'll miss it.

Okay, I'll miss some of it. I'll miss the women and the dancing, but not the drinking or the smoking or my swollen, bruised, sore knees - or my escalating feelings of paranoia.

I won't miss feeling so completely out of control. I'm looking forward to getting my life back. Of course, I can't keep this up any longer, and it's not like I can afford to quit my day job. The Seattle area is expensive, even the outlying suburbs are expensive. I don't really have a choice, I have to commit to my grown up career or fail to make my rent and risk losing my still unsold house back home.

I find Michael and let him know that I need to quit, my last day is two weeks from tonight. He says he understands, but that if I ever want to come back, it'll be just fine with him.

"We need more dancers like you. You've always got a smile on your face. You sit down with the customers and make them feel welcome. That goes a long way here."

"Thanks. I appreciate that. I've enjoyed working here, but I'm just too tired to keep up."

Michael gives me a hug.

"Good luck to you."

Well, at least that's over with. No hard feelings. I'll lay low, make the most of the next two weeks, have fun, make money and go right back to my life. No harm, no foul.

I change into my costume and then head for the bar. Paul serves me gin and tonic number one.

"So I hear you are leaving us. What's up with that? I thought you loved it here?" He's mocking me, but I'm used to it.

"I know, I know."

"So what are you going to do?"

"I'm going to concentrate on my day job."

"Has it gotten any better for you there?"

"No, not really, but I'm still looking for something else. I can't keep up the pace of working both jobs anymore. I'm exhausted. I feel like shit, and I can barely walk."

"We'll miss you, but you weren't really a stripper anyway, right?"

"Well, I have been known to hop up on that stage right over there and take my shirt off, but yeah, it's just a hobby." I finally get a laugh out of him.

"How is the book coming?"

"I haven't started putting it all together yet, I've been too busy here, but I'm working on it. Hold on, I'll be right back, I want to get you something."

"Where am I going to go? I work here," he mutters. I ignore him and run to the dressing room, dig in my purse and pull out my business card. I write my phone number on it to give to him.

"You weren't kidding, you really have a Ph.D."

"At least that's what my business card says. I want to stay in touch, okay?" I'm hesitant, because I'm not sure if he likes me or only tolerates me. It's hard to tell with Paul.

"You're a nut, you know that?" He smiles and shakes his head.

Marcus announces it's time for the Zoot Scoot/shift change.

"Make sure you get a private dance from that special girl! Don't forget to tip your waitress. Hold on to your hats 'cause we've got the Zoot Scoot coming right up!"

I take my last swallow of my drink, hand the glass back to Paul and head for the stage. Yuck, I won't miss doing the Zoot Scoot.

Whoever steps onto the stage first for the Zoot Scoot, the DJ picks to be the first girl in rotation. No one wants to go first. It's early so the customers (and their money) are scarce. New dancers don't know this, and there is almost always at least one new girl, so the rest of us hang back and busy ourselves until one of them gets on stage for the Zoot Scoot first. Call it a rite of passage.

I'm the third dancer to set foot on the stage for the Zoot Scoot, so I'm third in the rotation. I'm wearing my favorite costume, a gold lamé halter and matching panels of sequined fabric that tie together to make a skirt. Kara puts her hand out to me to trade the stage, and I climb the steps to Stage One. As I stand there waiting for my music to start, I look over at Paul from behind the bar. I catch his eye for just a second, as he looks up to hand a customer a drink.

The music starts, but I don't sway to it or even move at all. I'm not even sure if I hear it. I'm still staring at Paul. He knows I'm a fraud. I'm the one who told him. He knows I'm not really a stripper. I know I'm not really a stripper, so what the hell am I doing up here?

I look down at my feet. I've forgotten how to dance. I shake my head clear and for the next 10 minutes, I fake it. It was as though someone reached down and snatched my ruby stripper slippers. Just like that, Oz turned right back into Kansas.

Wild and Crazy Librarians

If you are not free to choose wrongly and irresponsibly, you are not free at all.

> — *Jacob Hornberger, defeated United States Senate Independent Candidate for Virginia (2002)*

"Mom?" I traverse the obstacle course of halfway-unpacked boxes that are still scattered all over the living room.

"Yeah, babe, I'm home."

"How was your day?" My daughter asks me this everyday when I get home from work because my answer is always the same and it always makes her laugh.

"It sucked monkey poop just like yesterday. How was your day?"

"Pretty good. I got a 95 on my science test, want to see it?"

"Yeah, let me see it." Maria digs through her backpack for the graded test and hands it to me. It's the entire skeletal system, very impressive.

"Some guy came to the door for you today."

"Who?"

"He said he was a friend of yours. I wasn't going to let him in, but dad started talking to him."

"What did he look like? Was he tall with glasses? Light brown hair?"

"Yeah, Steve, right?"

"What happened? What did he say?"

"I don't know. He's your friend. He said he just wanted to stop by and see if you were here. He wanted to meet us. He works at your office, right?"

"Yes. He works in my building." I lie.

"Him and dad starting talking about the librarian party."

"The librarian party? The libertarian party?" My heart is pounding wondering what the hell went on here today, and they were talking politics.

143

"Yeah, the libertarian party. That guy is weird. He's all trying to talk to me and asking me how my "mommy" is doing. Why doesn't he just talk to you at work?"

"I don't know. Did he stay long?"

"Not that long. Him and dad just talked about that, and they talked about stuff to do in the city. Then dad started telling him about the dogs, and how we can't find a place to live that'll let us take them. You know how dad is, I think he got bored because he left pretty soon after that."

"Where's dad now?"

"I think he went to the grocery store to get us stuff for dinner."

What the hell, why didn't he just invite him to dinner? I call him on the cell phone; he's picking up Dmitri at school and stopping at the grocery store on the way home. I don't want to freak him out, so I wait until he gets home to explain.

"Do you know who that was today?"

"He works at your office, right? Seems like a nice guy, kind of dorky though. He has a crush on you, doesn't he?"

"That was that guy — the one from the club — the one who's been hanging around me."

"That's him? How does he know where you live?"

"I don't know, but don't let him in next time, okay?"

"I won't. What is going on with this guy? Should I be worried?"

"Worried like I might run off with him or worried that he might ax murder us?"

"Either."

"Well, I can say for sure that I'm not going to run off with him."

"Should we do something about this?"

"I don't know, what could we do? Did he seem scary to you?"

"No, actually, not at all. I thought he was one of those interns from your office. He said he gave you a ride home after work once, and he was nearby and thought he'd just stop by and see if you were home."

"What else?"

"He talked to Maria a little, I told him about the bullshit with the dogs. Then he said he had to get going and he left."

"That's it?"

144

"That was it. What's else is going on with this?"

"Nothing really. I'm just freaked about him getting my address and coming here. I think if he comes around any of us again, we should ask him to stop, and if it gets any worse, I guess we should call the police. Although I haven't a clue what we would say. Some man is coming around, buying food for strippers and making pleasant conversation?"

"Do you feel threatened?"

"Not really, but this is creepy and wrong." I didn't tell him about the flowers and the necklace before this, because I thought it would blow over, and I can't tell him now or he'll think I was trying to hide it from him.

"So what do you want to do?" he asks.

"I don't think there is anything we can do unless he shows up again. He hasn't given me any reason to get a bouncer or anybody else involved, but if I see him again, I'll make it clear that he is making me uncomfortable and if he doesn't stop, I don't know, I'll get a protection order."

"I don't want you to go back there again. You've already quit, just stop going."

"I can't do that. I still have a week left."

"So? You can't keep going there with this wacko following you around. They'll understand."

"I don't want to just stop going! I want to say goodbye."

"I understand that, but I don't think this is safe for you. It isn't fair to us for you to keep going there."

"I'll do one more shift, say goodbye to everybody, and that'll be it."

"You promise?"

"I promise."

My Big Exit

Here's a rule I recommend: Never practice two vices at once.
— *Tallulah Bankhead*

Tips In: $84
Tips Out: $0
Ransom for costume: $20

The dreaded third drink. If you recall, two drinks are my limit. The first one loosens me up. The second gets me feeling good, but without that tempting complete loss of control. The third drink transports me to another dimension — the third drink zone. When I consume drink number three, I have only one goal, one defining purpose — to drink more. I consume additional alcoholic beverages so fervently and so quickly that by the time someone catches on and cuts me off, it is far, far too late.

My final shift, a Saturday night, could have proven to be extremely profitable and I had planned to milk it for all it was worth. I've been a model employee and Michael, who appreciated my enthusiasm and positive attitude, said I could come back anytime I wanted to. It was sweet.

I had made it through my topless existential journey without being caught. I figured I'd get through this night, hang up my T-bar, and be home free. I'd dance my little heart out, have a wonderful time, say goodbye to my friends and take home a big, fat pile of money. This was how I planned to end my story. Good girl gets naked, but comes out on top. In my ever present compulsion for high achievement, if somewhat skewed in this case, I wanted to retire not only unscathed, but oh-so fabulous.

I had such high hopes for this night, all of which were thwarted by the dreaded "Drink Number Three".

I get in early, too early to start my shift so I buy a pack of cigarettes to share and sit at the bar to drink. Lydia and a young girl I've never met before come to sit by me. They don't know I am leaving.

147

"Why are you quitting? We have so much fun. Are you going to another club?"

"My legs are killing me. I can barely walk every morning after a shift. Ladies, I am too old for this, plain and simple. I can't continue going at this pace, and I can't afford to quit my day job. Plus I miss my kids."

"Oh you are not that old, you look good. How old are your kids?"

"Sixteen and twelve."

"No way, are they your step kids?"

"No, they're both mine. They both came out of my vagina. I remember it very well." While I am always flattered when people express a belief that I am far too young to have teenage children, I can't seem to help myself when someone asks if they are mine. Lydia and the new girl laugh at my crudeness and bum a couple cigarettes from me.

"See, I told you. You move around too much. You wear yourself out in the first set. You have to pace yourself and not dance so much." This is true. I loved to jump around all over the place. I maul that stage and have so much fun doing it, but I always pay later. It certainly has caught up with me.

Last Sunday my family went to the Old Spaghetti Factory that has a section built inside to look like a train car. My kids wanted to sit there so we had to wait for ages to get a table. I didn't notice the stairs leading up into it, walking up stairs was not a problem, but when we finished our meal and it was time to leave, I hovered at the top of the stairs dreading how it would feel to step down each one. Sheer agony. Luckily, neither of my kids noticed the grimace on my face as I made my stiff-legged descent.

Marcus calls me up to the DJ booth.

"So what's the deal? I thought next Saturday was your last day."

"Something came up at home. You know how it is."

"You bet I do. Well, that's too bad. I'll miss ya, honey."

"Awwww, I'll miss you too." He puts his mammoth arms around me and gives me a big hug, not missing an opportunity to squeeze my butt one more time before I go. He's not subtle, but he is sincere. When I step out of the booth, Stephen is standing there waiting for me.

"Hi."

"Hi, yourself."

Stephen motions for me to sit down, "Let's sit, ok?"

"Let me just get this out right now. You're scaring the shit out of me."

"I know. I'm sorry."

"How did you get all my personal information?"

"I paid a bouncer to get it out of your personnel file."

"Fuckers."

"Yeah."

"How much? Oh, never mind, I don't want to know."

"I'm sorry I scared you. I really did not mean to."

"Well, you did. My husband thought you were pretty nice though." I was about to tell him that Maria thought he was goofy, but thankfully, I stopped short.

"I wanted to see if you were telling me the truth, you know, about being married and all. I thought maybe you were just saying that to get rid of me. You're family seems nice."

"They are nice."

"I guess I expected something different. You really are somebody's mother."

"Oh yeah. Some days more than others!"

"So have you figured out what you're going to do about all those dogs? Have you found a new place to live that will accept them?"

I laugh. The whole moving-with-three-dogs thing has truly taken on a life of it's own.

"No, we still don't know what we're going to do. We're trying to buy a house, but until the house back in Tucson sells, we're kind of stuck."

"Ahh." Stephen nods.

"I guess I didn't expect your apartment to be so regular, uh, normal, except really messy." I guess strippers live in ultra modern, specially appointed apartments in which every room is a boudoir, littered with bon bon wrappers, lingerie, and pink feather boas.

"Why don't you unpack?"

Good question. I change the subject, "So, this is my last night."

"I didn't know that. So, you're just going to keep the day job?"

149

"Yes. All of this is getting to be too much for me to handle. I do like working here, but I can't handle working this much and being away from my kids."

"That's sort of what I wanted to talk to you about. I really do care about you, if things were different, I would want to be with you. I mean, I do want to be with you, but I'm not the kind of person who goes around breaking up families."

"No, I understand. I didn't think you were."

"Well, I wish it could be different."

"That's nice of you to say." Okay, I don't want to sound too happy about this, but I don't want him to change his mind either. I'll miss the roses though, that was really cool.

"I've enjoyed knowing you. You're a very sweet guy." I smile at Stephen and give him a goodbye hug.

"But you should stop hanging out in strip clubs."

"You, too."

I made my way back to my gals who were, as usual, in the smoking room. Annabel passed by the three of us hanging around, as the kids say, smoking and joking. She looked me up and down and with an exaggerated look of concern on her face mouthed words to me, "You don't smoke!"

Since I only smoke inside the club and this is my last night, I wasn't worried about kicking my new old bad habit. Smoking is not attractive, especially on me, and I would catch hell if anyone at home were to find out. Dismissive, I waved Annabel off and started sucking back my second gin and tonic. After managing to throw on a costume, I found some of my regulars and had a seat. Miranda came over to wait on us. Apparently she was unaware of my self-imposed two-drink limit and brought me a third drink and without bothering to ask me first, she made it a double.

"Don't worry, I'll keep an eye on you. I won't let you get too drunk." Famous last words. That makes four, with no food in my stomach. I'll never know for certain whether she got me plastered on purpose.

I can tell you what I remember. I was dancing on Stage Two and some frat boys signaled for me to come over to their end of the stage. One of them was twenty-one today, and they asked me about buying a birthday dance. The birthday boy sits on a chair in the middle of the stage, where no less than three girls dance for him. The dancers get a minimum of twenty dollars each, so I wanted in on it. I leaned down toward the young men, "I'll tell you how to buy one as long as you choose me as one of the dancers.

"Of course!"

"Just go up to the DJ booth, Marcus is there, he'll set you up."

Lydia, Annabel and I circled him as he sat in his chair in the middle of the stage. He was cute, and I was so drunk. When it was my turn to dance for him, I straddled his lap and planted a long, hard kiss on him. Annabel yanked me off him and tried to keep going as though nothing had happened, but I guess I did it again. When the birthday dance was over, I started making out with him. Kurt pulled me into the DJ booth and explained that this was against the rules. Further, I was obviously intoxicated, and he could not allow me to remain on the dance list. He sent me to the dressing room to sober up.

I remember sitting on the floor of the dressing room negotiating with Micki to buy back some of my "misplaced" costumes. I had let Pandora snag some of my favorite costumes and although I can't imagine why I needed them back, I offered twenty dollars to whomever returned them to me, no questions asked — not that I was in any shape to interrogate. My black vinyl outfit turned up, but no one seemed to know where my thigh-high boots were so I scrawled out a note describing them with my phone number and taped it to the mirror.

Trying to get a dancer's attention, I kept calling out, "Tara! Tara!" trying to get this woman, whose name was apparently not Tara, to turn around.

"Are you trying to talk to me?"

"Yes."

"My name is not Tara. What do you want?"

I wanted to talk to her because I had heard that her father was a professor of statistics at a prestigious university. In my altered state, I must have thought he could get me a job there. In a pathetic attempt to impress her or get some attention, I gave her my card. She looked at it and said, "What the hell are you doing working here?"

"I thought it would be fun." Sometime after this conversation, I collapsed in a heap on the dressing room floor, but did manage to become increasingly loud and obnoxious. Before I knew it, Kurt was escorting me out of the dressing room. The other girls had complained about me and wanted me out of there. Kicked out of the dressing room, I told Kurt that I was much too drunk to drive home. I needed to sit down somewhere. Kurt put me in the ladies lounge and I can only assume that I fell asleep in the tall wing back chair.

I wanted to make a splashy exit, but this was not at all what I had in mind. I was so drunk that I didn't even know enough to be embarrassed by my behavior. Not yet anyway. After what I guess to be about an hour, I emerged from the lounge intent on getting myself home. I was still too wobbly to make the drive so I decided to call my husband to come get me. Before I dialed the phone I saw him sitting there, scanning the room looking for me.

Allan had come to see me dance. He stayed away before now because he knew it would make me nervous, but he wanted to see me dance before it was too late. I had screwed up, and now it was too late. All this time Allan had been sitting at a table fending off opportunistic dancers while waiting for me to show up on stage. He saw my car in the parking lot and became understandably very concerned when he didn't see me anywhere in the club.

"I'm sorry. Please take me home, I'll explain in the car." Allan drove us home in my car, but I didn't feel much like talking.

Dear C*nts,

On a personal level, freaking out is a process whereby an individual casts off outmoded and restricting standards of thinking, dress, and social etiquette in order to express creatively his relationship to his immediate environment and the social structure as a whole.

— Frank Zappa

I slept a long, long time. I had the whole Sunday to rest before I had to go back to my real job. As far as I can tell, no one knows. If they did, what would they say? I've made a decision to try to get along and do the best job I can, but keep looking for something else.

Lynne makes her usual rounds at ten and two, she checks in on me to ask me how it's going. During one of her stops in my office, she noticed the framed poster that had been propped against my office wall. After so many months, I still had yet to hang it. It's a picture with all kinds of symbols, a peace sign, a Star of David, a pink triangle, symbols of organized labor and feminism. I ordered it years ago from a hippie catalog. Below the symbols is a statement, translated and paraphrased from Dante's Inferno, "The hottest places in hell are reserved for those who, in times of great moral crisis, maintain their neutrality." Lynne looks the poster up and down and then looks at me.

"You don't really believe that do you?" She asked. I looked at the floor, "I used to," I said.

I'm short on billable hours, and I know from experience that if I don't make some work to do now, I'll be suffering a lecture or whatever punishment Lynne has cooked up for me this month. Dan sends a little my way, but it seems harder for him to explain to me whatever he needs than to just do it himself. I go to Lynne, but she just routs me right back to Dan.

There is nothing for me to do, but I feel like I can't leave the sauna I call my office. I won't hear a peep from anyone in days, but the last time I left early, I came back the next day to a phone message from Lynne wondering where I'd been. Monday through Thursday, I sit like a hostage behind my desk. Until Friday of course, when

153

inevitably Lynne finds a pile of work for me to do that absolutely has to be done for Monday.

"The lawyers have to have it by Monday, so I need it before then. You know how it is." So I sit, bored and trapped Monday through Thursday. Then crazy busy all weekend with an urgent project, each time Lynne would insist she could not have given me even one minute sooner. This goes on for weeks. I feel like I never have a whole day off. I'm an exposed nerve. Finally, one Saturday afternoon, I'm logged in as usual and Lynne sends me an email.

"Are you online?"

I should have known not to answer. I should have known better. But no, I was working and I was online and goddamn if I wasn't going to let her know it.

"Yes."

"What are you working on?"

"I'm writing the shells of the program so that as soon as I get the data, I can get started."

"Who told you to do that?"

Oh Jesus. I can't deal with this anymore. Don't answer her. Just don't answer her. I can feel my chest tightening and my face getting hot. Dan, my immediate supervisor told me to do that, and if I don't do it now, if I wait until I get the data, I'll be working on this all night. The two of them have been volleying me back and forth since I took this stupid job. I can't help myself. I answer her. I answer her and I copy everyone else, including Dick.

"I'm writing the program now, because if I don't, I'll be working on this project all night. I've got to have some time to help my family settle in."

She answers back, replying to all, "Cheryl, if you need some time, go ahead and take it. I'll talk to Dan about getting this done."

That was it. I should have gotten up and unpacked some boxes, taken a walk, made scrambled eggs for everybody — anything but write another email. So of course, I wrote another email, this time to Dick. I'll spare you the gory details. Suffice it to say, I laid it all out there, simultaneously bitching at him and begging him for some help dealing with my dueling bosses. Within twenty minutes, I had an answer.

In a nutshell, his reply was, "Fuck you" but slightly longer, more eloquent and without the actual F-word.

I furiously constructed my response. A two-page letter telling him all about the horse he rode in on, wrapping it all up with an ironic use of "Mazel Tov!" It was a career ending email. If I had been in my right mind, I might have been worried about it. About a half hour later, Dan calls to tell me that, thanks to my antics, he has been fired.

That's when I lost it. We had just put down first and last months rent down on a house so that we could get our dogs back with us. I still had two months rent left to pay on this apartment and because my house back in Tucson hadn't sold, I continue to pay the mortgage on that, too. Now our only income was gone, without even two weeks notice, and I had just gotten my boss fired. What am I going to tell my kids? How am I going to get us back home?

I go to the bathroom to cry until I can barely open my swollen eyes. Exactly how many lives can I ruin with my stupidity? How the hell did I let things get so far out of control? Exhausted and dehydrated, I walk to the kitchen to get some water and on my way back through the dining area, next to some recently opened moving boxes, I see a box cutter.

Later the same year, box cutters would become notorious as the weapon used to hijack a plane during the September 11 attacks. I see it and remember Hope and her box cutter. No one sees me take it into the bathroom with me.

I stare at myself in the mirror, crying, puffy and red-faced. How the hell did I let this happen? I am not the kind of person who tells people off and quits her job! I do not throw a fit and leave without notice, with no reserved savings, for God's sake! Burning bridges! Getting people fired? I don't do things like that, that's not who I am.

I stare at the dull silver box cutter for what seems like half an hour, holding it against my wrist. Thinking about whether I have the guts to make the vertical incisions necessary to bleed to death in the bathtub, like I have seen before in movies. I sit there staring at it so long, that finally, through my sobbing, I laugh out loud at the prospect of me going through with it.

STRIPPER SHOES

Let's pretend just for the sake of argument that I am able to make two deep cuts in my left wrist. Then I would have to use my left hand, bleeding profusely from the wrist, to cut into my right one. That is just *not* going to happen. Maybe you don't have to cut both wrists? I wonder about these details long enough to break out of the crescendo of my melodrama and start thinking about more practical matters. Maybe I can go in on Monday and fix this somehow. Maybe I can at least find a way to leave on better terms, work some of this out like mature adults.

Monday morning comes. I have had little sleep from fretting and crying, but I put myself together as best I can. Whatever happens, I want to look good while it is happening to me. Whatever dignity I can hold on to, I will. I know I can't stay on, too much has been said, in print no less, but if I can get two weeks pay and Dan's job back, I'll be grateful.

Dick will see me right way. Let's get this over with.

"Is there anything else you'd like to say?" He asks, politely waiting his turn to blast me.

"No, I think I covered it all in the email."

"Yes, you certainly did. Your email to me was arrogant and presumptuous. You don't know the first thing about me and your opinion on the way things ought to be is not appreciated."

"Look, you don't know what this has been like for me, and I know it doesn't make any difference now. I just need a little help getting home."

"How you get back to Tucson is not my problem."

"Well, then I guess I am under no obligation to continue this conversation."

I leave. I try my best not to cry as I pack up my things from my office, but of course I do. Allan helps me carry things out. I ignore the Daughters of Phorcys and Ceto as I walk in and out of the area, which isn't difficult because they are avoiding me, busily piecing the parts of the story together.

They give Dan another chance. He flies (first class) from the east coast to meet with all of them. Dan is asked to sit in a chair from 9 to 4:30 (with one 45 minute lunch break) during which time Dick and each of the Daughters come in, individually and in groups to tell him exactly what it is they don't like about him. To keep his job, he

156

agrees to listen quietly and not respond. I wonder what human resources handbook this technique came out of. Dan is also forced to agree to take some anger management classes and move to Washington to work in this office indefinitely.

Since my hasty departure (and possibly prior to it), Lynne rooted through every one of my emails left on the server until she found the perfect email string to finish us both off. I handed this one to her on a silver platter.

It went something like this:

Cheryl: Did those cunts ever tell you what we are supposed to be working on?
Dan: "Dear Cunts" Is that their official name?
Cheryl: No, officially, they are the "fucking, fat, barren, humorless, ugly cunts."
Dan: Thanks, I'll just copy and paste that.;)

He didn't know it yet, but Dan was fired (again and for good) before he even got off the plane back home. Lynne had read everything, any trace left behind like a ghost on my computer or on the server. I was too distraught to think about cleaning it and in some cases it was already too late. Emails left in my inbox for more the 24 hours had been automatically copied to the server. Emails I had written to family and friends, private thoughts, every communication.

She read it like a diary, claiming she had a right to go through everything in case I might have any sensitive information that could compromise a case. She knew I didn't, but it was a good enough excuse. I have never felt so violated, but there was nothing I could do but let it go. I heard from the few friendly acquaintances in the office that the Daughters read all about my moonlighting at Zoot Allures. I'm sure they've had more than a few laughs at my expense. I tell myself that I shouldn't care, but it is humiliating. Small consolation, however I took some comfort in knowing that I'd still rather be someone whose diary is read than someone who would stoop to read someone else's.

Is That A Lizard In Your Pocket Or Are You Just Glad To See Me?

If I had to live my life again, I'd make the same mistakes, only sooner.
— *Tallulah Bankhead*

Two months rent on lease: $2,400
Movers and rental truck: $6,100
Food, gas, and lodging: $275
Going home: Priceless

A crisis situation is when my husband, Allan, really shines. The trip home is one giant blur, but I have over $5,000 in moving charges on the American Express card to remind me. Allan scooped me up and piled us all into a moving truck, towing the car behind it. Throughout the two-day trip, I rationed and popped whatever pills I had left in my purse to help me stop crying.

Allan drove, and the kids and I squeezed together on the front bench seat. The poor dogs had to stay inside the truck, and we stopped every few hours to take them for a quick walk. We have a pet lizard, a bearded dragon, to be precise. It was still cold, and there was no where else to put him, so I kept him on my lap the whole way home so that he could take advantage of my body heat. Every few hours, I'd sob into his spiky little head and take another pill.

Though nearly bankrupt, I made it home, right back into our unsold house, poorer, but wiser. And thinner. I happily returned to my old job, but looking something like an academic refugee. We juggled bills, and I deferred my student loans until we got back on our feet. Recovery was slow, but I remembered to keep moving.

A Good Samaritan stripper saw the note I left taped to the mirror in the dressing room. She knew where my favorite black boots were and returned them to me. I gave her a small reward for her trouble that she didn't want to take, but I insisted.

I began writing from my notes, scribbled on napkins and scraps of wrinkled paper that I had stuffed along with dollar bills into my bag. I wish that I could say that I was as diligent in note taking as I had intended to be. Originally, I approached this as a researcher, intent on observing and recording as accurately, and as objectively as possible. However, one cannot step inside without in some way intruding on the experience, or avoid being affected by it. I was not casual and I am not detached. Before I knew it happened, I was *being* instead of studying, an experience too rare for me until now.

I was so unhappy, but I would have found a way to manage one way or another. I went along making all kinds of miserable decisions because my outer self did not seem to realize that I had a choice. Thank goodness my insides were unconvinced. Even if my intestines had to personally manufacture a chaotic, half-naked, socially unacceptable crossroads for me, they would not steer me wrong.

After that horrible email string was discovered, Dan became very depressed. He thought about starting his own practice, but ended up taking a consulting position with Dick's main competitor, with Dick's blessing. I think, by then, we all had greater clarity and perspective on the situation. It took me one year to forgive them, two years to forgive myself. We are all better off now than we were so what is the purpose of holding a grudge? Grudges cause wrinkles.

The email, now called FFBHUC, for short, cannot be glossed over without some comment. I've thought about that email many times since I wrote it. I wonder if Lynne sees those words scroll over her eyes whenever she can't sleep at night. I often do. Sometimes I feel vengeful, other times, sorry. When I tell the story, I usually leave out the word I feel most ashamed of, the one I'd take back if I could —
fat.

Intellectually, I know that I felt out of control and pushed too far and I lashed out with whatever I could, but I also know just how vicious that word is. When it's hurled, it is meant to hurt every bit as much as the words, kike, or nigger, or spic do. I meant to be cruel and I was, whether I feel justified on some level doesn't make me feel any less sorry.

In his new position, Dan was given greater responsibility and more flexibility and independence. Also, he nearly doubled his income. Dan bought a condo on the beach and the boat he'd always dreamed of. It was my fault he was fired, but his happier circumstances made it easy for him to forgive me.

As a family, we pretty much picked up right where we left off, back in our old house, the kids, back in their old schools. It took me a long while to build my confidence back up. I spent a lot of time wondering how I could have done things differently, wishing I had been more experienced and mature. As much as I regretted almost every step, I was better off for the journey. I learned more in the previous year than I had in the ten before it. I learned to listen to my intuition and to respect my own needs. I also learned to open my eyes and ears and pay more attention to the needs that others are trying to express.

With my ten years of compressed wisdom and newfound tolerance for risk, I started my own consulting practice, specializing in equal opportunity issues. Every now and then, I think about stripping again. It is usually after a long week behind a computer, when I can literally feel my muscle tone slipping away — too much in my mind, not enough in my body. I still have what's left of my costumes, but I'd need to dance at least a few weeks to fit back into them. I miss it, but I don't need it anymore.

I love what I do, and although I haven't quite decided yet how I feel about this, I can accomplish more with my brains than I can with my body. Regardless of what I do now, I know that I am a stronger, smarter, happier person for having walked a mile or two in sexy, dangerous shoes.

In the real, grown-up world of fully dressed people, I take back with me three important lessons, in no particular order: (a) men love tits; (b) do whatever you need to until someone tells you to stop; and (c) it's never too late to paint over yourself, take your turn on Stage One, and dance to music that you like.

EPILOGUE

Q: How many Jewish mothers does it take to change a light bulb?
A: None: "It's okay, I'll just sit here in the dark..."

Telling my kids about working as a stripper turned out not to be so bad. I got tired of minimizing my work on the computer screen every time they walked into the room, so one night I sat them down and blurted it out. Once I had convinced them that I wasn't kidding, they nodded and smiled supportively, then went back to watching TV.

Only very recently did I tell my parents. It was excruciating, but my mother said I was "gutsy", and my father carefully proofread my manuscript. A happy relief, the sky didn't fall in, as I had imagined it might.

Early on, I sought feedback from people whom I trusted to give me constructive feedback and whose writing skills I admired. It is a vulnerable position to be in, especially because I was writing about myself. It reminded me of being pregnant. Once you start to show, you become public domain. People seem to feel obligated to share with you gruesome pregnancy and childbirth stories. Also, the university is like a small town. When I handed over drafts for comments, I was very clear that I would prefer the contents be kept private.

The reactions of the few people I confided in fell into distinct categories. Either stripping was no big deal and I was a ninny for worrying about what my colleagues might think, or stripping was a colossal mistake and I had irreparably damaged my credibility, and ruined my career. One more thing that I learned from my experience — people will never fail to jump at the chance to tell you that you're screwed. A third category, and decidedly the worst, was one of no direct feedback to me, but much discussion to others, that eventually made its way back to me. After that, as one sympathetic friend put it, I had to write in the dark.

My silence was lifted for the first time recently when I joined a community service advisory board. As a "get to know you" exercise, the chairperson asked that each of us write anonymously on a sheet of

163

paper the wildest thing we have ever done. When all the slips of paper were collected, we were to guess which wild admission belonged to whom. I hadn't even told my best friend yet, but without a second's hesitation, I wrote, *I once worked as a stripper* and passed the paper forward.

Only after the third try did someone guess that the former stripper was me. I have to admit, I was somewhat disappointed that I wasn't the obvious choice. Other than "Really?" there wasn't much commentary until after the meeting, when the chairperson spoke to me privately. She asked me some questions about what it was like, and if I wouldn't mind volunteering with a program to help improve the health and quality of life of local prostitutes. She felt that my experiences might provide a unique insight that could be useful.

Insight. What is my insight? I've spent so many hours trying to figure out what this book, what this experience, was about, but until right then, I wasn't sure. This book is about dancing, and about dancers, but it's also about determination, and about me. If I have something to say to prostitutes, it would be the same thing that I would say to anyone. If you feel stuck, find ways to get unstuck. If the first thing you try doesn't work, try something else. No matter how many people tell you that you're screwed, don't give up. And when you finally get unstuck, it will be worth it.

REFERENCES

Foote, N. (1954). Sex as play. *Social Problems, 1,* 159-163.

Forsyth, C. & Deshotels, T. (1997). The occupational milieu of the nude dancer. *Deviant Behavior, 18* (2), 125-142.

Holsopple, K. (1998). Stripclubs according to strippers: Exposing wokplace violence. Retrieved Oct 10, 2001, from the University of Rhode Island, Women's Studies Web site: http://www.uri.edu/artsci/wms/hughes/stripc1.htm

Rambo Ronai, C. & Ellis, C. (1989). Turn-ons for money: Interactional strategies of the table dancer. *Journal of Contemporary Ethnography, 18* (3), 271-298.

Scott, D. (1996). *Behind the G-string: An exploration of the stripper's image, her person, and her meaning.* Jefferson, NC: McFarland & Co.

RULES

1. ANYONE FOUND IN POSSESSION OF ILLEGAL DRUGS ON ▮▮▮▮▮▮▮ PROPERTY WILL BE FIRED AND 86'D. THIS INCLUDES ANYONE CONSPIRING TO AID IN THE SALE OR PURCHASE OF ILLEGAL DRUGS.

2. YOU ARE NOT ALLOWED TO LEAVE THE BUILDING DURING YOUR SHIFT UNLESS YOU HAVE PERMISSION FROM THE MANAGER AND AN ESCORT. IF THIS RULE IS VIOLATED WE WILL HAVE TO ASSUME THAT YOU WERE ENGAGING IN SOME FORM ILLEGAL ACTIVITY. THIS WILL RESULT IN YOU BEING FIRED AND 86'D.

3. SOLICITING ACTS OF PROSTITUTION IS ILLEGAL AND WILL RESULT IN YOUR BEING FIRED AND 86'D .

4. IF YOU ARE FOUND TO BE EXPOSING YOUR GENITALIA OR PUBIC HAIR TO CUSTOMERS AND/OR ARE FOUND TO BE TOUCHING CUSTOMERS AND/OR ALLOWING CUSTOMERS TO TOUCH YOU IN A MANOR THAT IS DEEMED INAPPROPRIATE OR ILLEGAL, YOU WILL BE FIRED AND 86'D.

5. IF YOU ARE 21 YEARS OF AGE OR OLDER AND IF YOU HAVE YOUR I.D. BEHIND THE BAR YOU MAY DRINK ALCOLHOL IN MODERATION. YOU CANNOT DRINK TO A STATE OF DRUNKENESS. ALL DRINKS MUST REMAIN ON THE FLOOR AND YOU CANNOT TAKE ALCOHOLIC DRINKS IN THE LADIES ROOM OR THE DRESSING ROOM AT ANY TIME.
        YOU MAY NOT DRINK STRAIGHT SHOTS OR SHOOTERS OR ANY DRINKS CONTAINING MORE THAN ONE SHOT OF ALCOHOL (I.E. LONG ISLAND ICE TEAS OR ZOMBIES). VIOLATION OF THESE RULES COULD RESULT IN THE SUSPENSION OF DRINKING PRIVILAGES OR SUSPENSION FROM WORK. REPEAT OFFENDERS COULD LOSE THEIR JOB.

6. IT IS ILLEGAL TO BRING ALCOHOL INTO WORK. IF YOU ARE FOUND TO BE BRINGING YOUR OWN ALCOHOL TO WORK YOU WILL BE FIRED AND 86'D.

7. ANYONE UNDER 21 YEARS OF AGE CAUGHT WITH OR FOUND TO BE UNDER THE INFLUENCE OF ALCOHOL AT WORK WILL BE FIRED AND 86'D. THIS ALSO APPLIES TO ANYONE OVER 21 FOUND TO BE FURNISHING ALCOHOL TO A MINOR.

8. WHILE YOU ARE EMPLOYED AT ▮▮▮▮▮. YOU ARE NOT ALLOWED TO PERFORM ANY ADULD ENTERTAINMENT OUTSIDE THE CLUB. SOME EXAMPLES WOULD BE BACHELOR PARTIES, STRIP-O-GRAMS, OUT CALL DANCE OR MASSAGE SERVICES OR OTHER CLUBS WHICH FEATURE DANCERS. VIOLATORS WILL BE FIRED AND 86'D.

9. IT IS ILLEGAL TO ASK A CUSTOMER TO BUY YOU A DRINK. DOING SO CONSTITUTES AN ACT OF SOLICITING AND NOT ONLY COULD IT COST YOU YOUR JOB BUT IT CAN GET YOU ARRESTED. IT IS HOWEVER O.K. TO ACCEPT IF THE CUSTOMER OFFERS AND YOU ARE 21 OR OVER AND YOUR I.D. IS BEHIND THE BAR.

10. YOU ARE NOT PERMITTED TO DATE CUSTOMERS OR OTHER EMLPOYEES. IF YOU ARE DATING A CO-WORKER, ONE OF YOU MIGHT BE DISMISSED. IF YOU ARE DATING A CUSTOMER, YOU COULD BE DISMISSED OR THE CUSTOMER COULD BE BARRED FROM THE CLUB WHILE YOU ARE WORKING.

167

11. HUSBANDS AND BOYFRIENDS MAY COME IN FOR A FEW MINUTES (15-20) IF THEY ARE DROPPING YOU OFF. THEY MAY ALSO ARRIVE A HALF AN HOUR BEFORE YOU GET OFF WORK, HOWEVER THEY MAY NOT HANG OUT DURING YOUR SHIFT.

12. DO NOT SIT IN A CUSTOMERS LAP.

13. DO NOT KISS A CUSTOMER ON THE MOUTH.

14. YOU CANNOT USE YOUR MOUTH TO TAKE A TIP IF THE CUSTOMER IS TOUCHING IT.

15. TIPS CAN ONLY BE TAKEN ON THE HIP. YOU CANNOT TAKE TIPS IN THE FRONT OR THE BACK OF YOUR COSTUME, NOR CAN YOU TAKE TIPS IN YOUR TOP.

16. YOU CANNOT TAKE TIPS AND PULL THEM THROUGH THE BACK OF YOUR COSTUME, NOR IS IT ALLOWED TO PICK UP TIPS WITH YOUR REAR.

17. YOU MUST COVER YOUR BREASTS AND REAR COMPLETELY WHEN NOT ON STAGE. YOUR NIPPLES CANNOT BE VISIBLE THROUGH LACE OR TRANSPARENT MATERIALS AND YOU MUST HAVE A SKIRT OR SOMETHING ON THOSE LINES TO COVER THE CLEFT OF THE BUTTOCKS.

18. YOU'RE REQUIRED TO WEAR SHOES AT ALL TIMES. THE ONLY EXCEPTIONS WILL BE DURING THE LAST SONG OF YOUR SET IF YOU ARE DOING SOMETHING GYMNASTIC OR PERFORMING A FLOOR SHOW. YOU MUST HOWEVER STILL HAVE SOCKS OR FOOTIES ON YOUR FEET.

19. AT NO TIME CAN YOU TOUCH YOUR BREASTS OR CROTCH WHILE PERFORMING, NOR CAN YOU SIMULATE ANY SEX ACTS SUCH AS ORAL SEX OR MASTERBATION. NOT ONLY WILL YOU JEOPARDIZE YOUR JOB BUT YOU COULD ALSO GET ARRESTED.

20. ANYTIME THERE IS AN ALL DANCE YOU ARE EXPECTED TO BE ON STAGE UNLESS YOU HAVE A TABLE DANCE. WHILE YOU ARE ON STAGE (WEATHER IT BE AN ALL DANCE OR NOT) YOU ARE EXPECTED TO BE DANCING AND NOT SITTING OR STANDING AROUND. ALSO DRINKING AND SMOKING ON STAGE IS STRICTLY PROHIBITED.
 YOU MUST ALSO CONDUCT YOURSELF PROFESSIONALY WHEN DOING YOUR REGULAR SETS, REGARDLESS OF WEATHER YOU ARE BEING TIPPED, WHAT MUSIC IS BEING PLAYED OR IF NO ONE IS SITTING AT YOUR STAGE. YOU STILL HAVE TO DANCE AND YOU STILL HAVE TO REMOVE YOUR TOP ON THE LAST SONG. VIOLATING THIS RULE COULD RESULT IN SUSPENSION FROM WORK.

21. PLEASE DRESS IN AN APPEALING AND SEXY MANOR. OUR CUSTOMERS WOULD STAY AT HOME IF THEY WANTED TO SEE A GIRL DRESSED LIKE AN OLD HOUSEWIFE.

22. ALL GIRLS ARE EXPECTED TO MOVE AROUND AND MEET DIFFERENT CUSTOMERS DURING THEIR SHIFT. DON'T WASTE YOUR TIME ON GUYS WHO DON'T WANT TABLE DANCES AND WHO DON'T TIP. YOU'RE HERE TO MAKE MONEY AND NOT TO MEET THE CUTE GUYS. REMEMBER CUSTOMERS WILL TIP YOU MORE IF THE FEEL THAT THEY KNOW YOU THAN IF YOU ARE A STRANGER.

23. DON'T HANG OUT IN THE DJ BOOTH OR THE LOBBY. YOU ARE HERE TO ENTERTAIN THE CUSTOMERS, NOT THE DJ OR THE DOORMEN.

24. ONLY ONE DANCER IS ALLOWED IN THE DJ BOOTH AT ONE TIME.

25. USE THE STAIRS WHEN GOING TO THE DRESSING ROOM. PLEASE DO NOT CLIMB ON THE RAILS.

26. AT CLOSING TIME ALL DANCERS MUST GO STRAIGHT TO THE DRESSING ROOM AND STAY THERE UNTIL THE DRESSING ROOM IS CLEANED AND UNTIL ALL THE CUSTOMERS HAVE LEFT THE BUILDING.

27. YOU MUST ARRANGE YOUR TRANSPORTATION AHEAD OF TIME. YOU MAY NOT LEAVE WITH THE CUSTOMERS. ALSO YOU MAY NOT HANG OUT IN THE PARKING LOT AFTER HOURS. YOU MUST VACATE THE LOT PROMPTLY.

28. DURING YOUR SHIFT YOU MAY USE THE DRESSING ROOM TO FRESHEN UP AFTER YOUR SET, HOWEVER THIS SHOULD NOT TAKE YOU MORE THAT 10 MINUTES (THE LENGTH OF TWO SONGS). YOU CAN'T MAKE ANY MONEY IN THE DRESSING ROOM, SO DON'T HANG OUT THERE.

29. IF YOU ARE NOT WORKING YOU ARE NOT ALLOWED IN THE DRESSING ROOM UNLESS YOU GET PERMISSION FROM THE MANAGER.

30. NON-EMPLOYEES ARE NOT ALLOWED IN THE DRESSING ROOM, SO LEAVE YOUR FRIENDS ON THE FLOOR.

31. GIRLS AUDITIONING SHOULD NOT BE LEFT ALONE IN THE DRESSING ROOM, IF YOU VALUE YOUR POSSESSIONS.

32. IF YOU STRIKE ANOTHER EMPLOYEE YOU WILL BE FIRED AND 86'D.

33. ALL DISPUTES BETWEEN EMPLOYEES SHOULD BE BROUGHT TO THE ATTENTION OF THE MANAGER. DO NOT MAKE MATTERS WORSE BY ARGUING WITH THE OTHER PERSON. THIS APPLIES TO PROBLEMS THAT YOU MAY HAVE WITH CUSTOMERS AS WELL.

I HAVE READ AND UNDERSTOOD THE RULES OF THE ███████ AND AGREE TO CONDUCT MYSELF IN ACCORDANCE WITH THESE RULES WHILE EMPLOYED AT THE ███████.

DATE

SIGNATURE_____

ABOUT THE AUTHOR

Cheryl Bartlett is the author of *Matriphobia: The Fear of Becoming One's Mother*, and *Feminist Theories: A Three Hour Tour*.

She earned her doctorate from the University of Arizona. Cheryl is the director of The Art of Science Research Support Services. She lives in Tucson, Arizona, where she still has not completely unpacked.

Printed in the United States
36668LVS00006B/145